engage

engage

A GUIDE TO CREATING
LIFE-TRANSFORMING WORSHIP SERVICES

nelson searcy
and jason hatley

WITH JENNIFER DYKES HENSON

BakerBooks

a division of Baker Publishing Group
Grand Rapids, Michigan

Published by Baker Books
a division of Baker Publishing Group
P.O. Box 6287, Grand Rapids, MI 49516-6287
www.bakerbooks.com

Printed in the United States of America

Library of Congress Cataloging-in-Publication Data
Searcy, Nelson.
      Engage : a guide to creating life-transforming worship services / Nelson Searcy and Jason Hatley, with Jennifer Dykes Henson.
            p.   cm.
      ISBN 978-0-8010-7217-8 (pbk.)
      1. Public worship—Planning. I. Hatley, Jason. II. Henson, Jennifer Dykes. III. Title.
      BV15.S43 2011
      264—dc23   2011017241

11   12   13   14   15   16   17   7   6   5   4   3   2

In keeping with biblical principles of creation stewardship, Baker Publishing Group advocates the responsible use of our natural resources. As a member of the Green Press Initiative, our company uses recycled paper when possible. The text paper of this book is composed in part of post-consumer waste.

To all the men and women we share the stage with each week
at
The Journey Church

contents

preface

*S*unday, *1:07 p.m.* Pastor Tim walks into his office, unbutton-
ing the top button of his shirt. He sets his Bible and notes
on his desk, sinks into his chair, and says a quick thank-you to
God for two great Sunday services. Tim hears a knock on his
door and looks up to see Scott, the worship pastor, poking his
head into the office.

"Just wanted to touch base before heading out," Scott says.

"Hey, Scott. Absolutely. Come on in." As Scott crosses to the
other chair, Tim continues, "I think the worship went really
well today."

"Yeah, thanks. It came together," says Scott, settling into the
chair with a sigh. "The message was powerful too."

"Well, thank you too," Tim says lightly. "God was definitely
moving."

"Definitely. What does your afternoon look like?" Scott asks.

"Lunch with the family and some friends who are in from out of town. Then I'm heading home for a long Sunday afternoon nap. You?"

"I'm going to get some rest too, but I need to start pulling a few things together for next week," Scott says.

"Yep, next Sunday will be here before we know it," Tim says.

"Sure will. And we'll do it all again," Scott answers. After a few silent moments, Scott says, "Well, I will see you in the office tomorrow morning."

"Sounds good, Scott. Enjoy your afternoon. See you tomorrow."

———

There's a fine line between Sunday afternoon and Monday morning. If you've been a teaching or worship pastor long, you know exactly what I mean. You spend all week planning, preparing, and praying for your Sunday services, and then, when they're over, you barely have a minute to breathe before it's time to start planning, preparing, and praying for the next week's services.

Sunday comes along with amazing regularity. Each time it gets here, you are expected to have biblical yet original material prepared for your attenders—something that will resonate with them and send them back into the world better than when they walked through your doors. You can't preach the same message you preached the week before; you can't sing the same songs; you can't show the same video clip or have the same guy give his testimony. The people sitting in front of you will be hungry for something fresh and new.

With this pressure on your shoulders, it's easy to fall into the trap of a Sunday-to-Sunday mentality—that is, to feel like you are just trying to get through the next Sunday, then the next

Sunday after that, then the next Sunday after that . . . constantly behind the eight ball and making it up as you go every week. Can you relate?

Here's some good news: you don't have to live and die by the weekly grind. You can break the week-to-week mentality that sabotages so many well-intentioned teaching and worship pastors. By putting a strong, biblically sound worship planning system in place, you will be able to maximize not only this Sunday but every single "next Sunday" to come. The key to getting out of the tailspin and cooperating with God to do church at a higher level can be summed up in one word: planning.

My prayer is that the principles and ideas contained within these pages will help you shake free from the stress of under-the-gun worship planning and discover the peace (not to mention the fruit!) that comes when you put a solid worship planning system to work in your church.

Let's get started—if you're not too tired!

introduction

engage |in-'gāj|: to attract and hold by influence or power : to interlock with : to cause to mesh.

Merriam-Webster

And let us not neglect our meeting together, as some people do, but encourage one another, especially now that the day of his return is drawing near.

Hebrews 10:25

The first church I pastored was a small Baptist church in Charlotte, North Carolina. I was a twenty-one-year-old kid. The night they voted to call me as pastor, a whopping fifteen people were in attendance. Later I learned the plan that night had been either to vote me in or to vote to merge with the church down the street. They went with me, but I'm still not sure they made the right decision. Fortunately, God began to bless that little church and it started to grow. After a few long, hard seasons, we were averaging almost one hundred people per week. Since attendance was so "high" every Sunday, I went to the deacon board with a proposal: we needed to hire a part-time minister of music. They reluctantly agreed.

After a few interesting interviews, I found a woman who fit the bill perfectly. Her name was Laura. Laura was an incredible singer, and her husband played the piano to boot—I got a two-for-one deal! Now, with the three of us on the platform, God began blessing our church even more. But things were far from perfect. The system I'm going to detail for you in the pages ahead had not yet formed in my mind, as was obvious by the ups and downs Laura and I struggled through. Here's what I mean:

Sunday morning would roll around, and Laura and I would both show up at church. Some Sundays the music would be focused on God's love, but my message would be an examination of God's wrath. Laura and I would meet at the altar after the service and shake our heads in frustration. Some Sundays we'd get to church and the music would be all about God's wrath (yes, there are a few in the Baptist hymnal), but my sermon would be on the sweetness of God's love. Once again, my new minister of music and I would meet at the altar, shake our heads, and sigh in frustration. But there were some Sundays—great, glorious, powerful Sundays—when the music would be about God's love and my sermon would be about God's love. Harmony! Bliss! Laura and I would meet at the altar and dance a little jig of celebration over how the Spirit had moved. (Good thing this didn't happen too often since we were in a Baptist church.)

After a few magnificent, "coincidental" Sundays when the music and the message matched, we came up with an idea. What if I would call Laura on Wednesday and tell her what I was planning to preach the following Sunday? Revolutionary, right? (Remember, I was only twenty-one. More advanced planning strategies had not yet penetrated my youthful cerebral cortex.) So Laura and I established a weekly phone call, during which I would explain my sermon topic so that she could select music and choir anthems accordingly. More and more often, we saw the Spirit move in our services. Amazing.

Thinking back on this early stab at creating powerful worship services makes me shudder, not just because my preaching was so bad (it was!), but also because I often blamed the Spirit for what was clearly a systems issue. My defunct worship planning was hindering God's Spirit from working at the highest level. I pointed a frustrated finger at the Spirit when I should have been pointing a finger at my own poor planning. Here's what I've since learned: the Holy Spirit is present in all our churches every Sunday, desiring to engage our hearts and change lives for the sake of Jesus Christ. Our worship planning systems will either complement or hinder the Spirit's work. The choice is ours: we can either cooperate with the Spirit or block his blessing. Which would you rather do?

Personally, I want to live every day of my life—and especially those days when I'm preaching God's messages—in harmony with God's Spirit! I want the Spirit to flow through our worship pastor and worship team, through our artistic worship expressions, and through the preaching of his Word. And I bet you do too! That's exactly what this book is designed to help you do. In the pages ahead, you will discover a worship planning system that you can adapt and use in your church to see results each and every Sunday, through the power of the Holy Spirit.

15

A Note on Systems

In case you aren't familiar with the concept of utilizing systems in your church, allow me to give you a brief overview. Those of you who are parents know the awe that comes with holding your newborn baby in your arms. Even though babies are born every day, each one is a miracle. Think back to the last time you looked at ten tiny fingers and toes or watched a little chest move up and down, drawing breath. By cliché, that baby is a bundle of joy, but she is also a bundle of something else. She is a bundle of perfectly formed, intricate systems that are already working together to keep her alive.

Thanks to her tiny circulatory system, her heart is pumping blood through her veins. Thanks to her respiratory system, her lungs are taking in air. Her digestive system is breaking down her mother's milk from the very first drop, and her muscular system is letting her wrap her little hand around her father's finger. Even in a brand-new baby, each of these systems and others are fully developed, fully functioning, and ready to grow with her as she starts her journey toward adulthood.

God is into systems. He organized the universe with systems. He established the measurement of time through a system. And, from the beginning, he formed our bodies as a cohesive unit of systems. Adam and Eve—unblemished specimens of God's craftsmanship—were compilations of the systems that caused them to function. They were perfect adult examples of that newborn baby. Without systems humming under the surface, they would not have been able to walk or even breathe. They wouldn't have been able to experience the pleasures of the garden. Without their systems, they would have remained unmolded lumps of clay, unable to fulfill the purposes of God. From the beginning, God has put systems to work, providing the mechanics and the platform through which he shows his greatness.

One more thing about Adam and Eve. What do we know about them for sure? What was the blueprint God used in creating them? Himself. Genesis affirms that God created man in his own image. Don't miss this: God created beings who function through systems and said that they were created in his own image. God is into systems.

Paul understood God's affinity for systems. That's why, in trying to help us wrap our minds around how the church should function, he compared the body of Christ to the human body. He aligned the design of the church with the functioning of our own different parts. In Romans, Paul writes, "Just as each of us has one body with many members, and these members do not all have the same function, so in Christ we, though many, form one body, and each member belongs to all the others" (12:4–5 NIV). Sounds remarkably like how God designed our physical bodies with systems, right? Go back and read the verse again substituting the word *systems* every time you see the word *members*. Makes perfect sense. All the parts of the body—both the church body and the physical body—work together, allowing us to fulfill God's purposes and plans on this earth. And both of those respective bodies function best through well-developed systems.

A system is any ongoing process that saves you stress, time, energy, and money and continues to produce results. Good systems function under the surface to keep things running smoothly so that you can concentrate on more important priorities. Thankfully, you don't have to think about the fact that your neurological system is allowing you to read and process this information.

That system is doing its job impeccably, or you wouldn't be able to understand the words in front of you. But if you begin to see a decline in your cognitive ability—if all of a sudden you cannot remember or analyze information in the way you always have—you will have to deal with the stress of knowing something is wrong and put a lot of money, time, and energy into figuring out where the breakdown is occurring. We may not be aware of a good system when it is running well, but there is no mistaking when something isn't working like it should.

The same is true in the church. We know that the church is a body, so it follows that the church also has systems working beneath the surface. I contend that the church is made up of eight systems: the worship planning system, the evangelism system, the assimilation system, the small groups system, the ministry system, the stewardship system, the leadership system, and the strategic system. (To learn more about all eight of these systems, download the free "Church Systems" report at www .ChurchLeaderInsights.com/Engage.)

Since my time at the little church in Charlotte, I've learned quite a bit about systems and how they hum beneath the surface of every thriving church. Each of the eight church systems is vitally important—a church couldn't be healthy with one missing any more than we could be healthy if one of our bodily systems shut down—but the worship planning system holds a key position in relation to the others. Our worship services are the front door through which people have the opportunity to enter into a relationship with Jesus and begin the journey toward becoming fully developing disciples. Each week, we work as co-laborers with the Holy Spirit to draw people to God for his glory. Without our worship services, our churches wouldn't exist. Without the worship planning system, there is no need for any of the other seven systems.

In 2002, my understanding of worship planning expanded exponentially. That's when I launched The Journey Church in New York City and began my partnership with Jason Hatley, The Journey's first pastor of worship arts. To this day, as my colleague and friend, Jason fills the same role with excellence. As you read *Engage*, you'll notice that it is written in my voice (Nelson Searcy). But I have to stress that, while I am the lead pastor of The Journey Church, the worship planning system you are about to discover is the result of a team effort. The lessons shared here have been equally developed through my ministry relationship and personal friendship with Jason. Jason is a musician, a strategist, an artist, a team builder, and a system designer. That's quite a package for one person. We both trust that you'll be able to benefit from our unique collaboration.

Throughout these pages, you'll have the opportunity to benefit from all that Jason and I have learned about worship planning the hard way. I trust that our struggle will enable you to implement a strong worship planning system more quickly than we did. Hopefully, our successes will be an encouragement to you—and proof that a high level of integrated, Spirit-driven planning is possible in your church too. I also like to think that all we've learned about relationships and teamwork throughout this process will be a model for you and your worship pastor. And perhaps our vocabulary will be embraced and implemented by your church as well. This book will teach you new words and phrases, such as preaching calendar, worship planning, creative planning meeting, message run-through, and the Thursday midnight rule. In the pages ahead, you'll discover:

- how to plan life-changing services each week
- how to ask the right questions before starting to plan
- how to break out of the cycle of stressful week-to-week planning
- how to utilize creative elements effectively
- how to bridge the common gaps between pastors and worship pastors
- how to develop a worship philosophy that both staff and volunteers can support
- how to evaluate and improve worship services each week
- how to plan months in advance for maximum impact
- how to (and why to!) develop a preaching calendar
- how to use the seasons of the year to maximize effectiveness
- how to create a culture of feedback based on common goals

You have a great journey ahead, as you prayerfully work through the pages in your hand. Thanks in advance for allowing God to use this book to speak to you, your pastor/worship pastor, and your worship team so that together we can all experience the full measure of what he wants to do in our churches each and every Sunday.

How to Get the Most out of This Book

1. Read with a pen in hand. Allow God's Holy Spirit to speak to you as you read, and capture the thoughts he brings to mind on paper.
2. Read with your worship pastor (or, if you are the worship pastor, read with your pastor). Take six weeks or so and make *Engage* the topic of your weekly meetings.

3. Share *Engage* with your teaching team, if you have one. Again, study the book over a set period with all your teaching pastors.

4. Take a season to study *Engage* with everyone who assists you in planning worship—both laity and ministers. I cannot overstate the value of having everyone on the same page when it comes to your worship philosophy and the resulting system.

5. Check out *Engage*'s website for additional information, free resources, downloads of documents included in the book, and more at www.ChurchLeaderInsights.com/Engage.

6. Share *Engage* with a fellow pastor—learn and return. Learn from the pages ahead and then return your knowledge to the kingdom by recommending *Engage* to someone else who may benefit from more engaged worship planning for more transforming worship services.

For God's glory, keep reading!

philosophy
of worship

1

why ask why?

Determining Your Philosophy of Worship

Philosophy, rightly defined, is simply the love of wisdom.

Cicero

If you are wise and understand God's ways, prove it by living
an honorable life, doing good works with the humility that
comes from wisdom.

James 3:13

Have you ever stopped to examine why you do things the way you do? I recently heard a story about a young, newlywed couple trying to navigate the intricacies of marriage several hundred miles from their families. One night, as the two were preparing dinner, the husband was peeling potatoes at the sink when he noticed his wife cutting the ends off the uncooked roast and throwing them away.

After she had seasoned the meat and put it in the oven, he asked her, "Why did you cut the ends off the roast? The ends are the best part."

Shooting him a don't-question-my-methods look, she answered, "Because. Well, just because . . . Actually, I'm not sure. That's the way my mom always does it."

Determined to save future end pieces and to get to the bottom of this mystery, the young man called up his mother-in-law and asked, "Why do you cut the ends off a roast before you cook it?"

The mother-in-law nonchalantly said, "I've just always done it that way. That's the way my mother did it."

Now the new husband was getting frustrated. Not willing to let the issue go, he put the mother-in-law on hold and called his new grandmother-in-law. When everyone was on the line together, he asked, "Grams, why do you cut the ends off a roast before you cook it?"

The grandmother gave a surprised laugh. "Because my pan is too small to fit a whole roast! Why do you ask?"

While tradition is generally a good thing, sometimes it can get us into trouble. If we aren't careful, we end up doing things a certain way simply because it's the way things have always been done. We never stop to question the mind-set behind the method. This is especially true when it comes to the way we plan and implement our worship services. We rarely pause to think about why we structure our time the way we do, why we have six songs instead of five, why we sing the style of songs we sing, why we have awkward silences during our transitions, why we receive the offering when, and how we do . . . You get the idea.

We get comfortable with the standard mode of operation and forget to ask the most important question we can ask: why?

You and I will never be able to reach the height of our effectiveness until we step back and examine why we do the things we do. Are you operating out of tradition, or are you working from a plan to create the best worship experiences possible and cooperate with God in transforming lives? To answer this question and move forward into God's highest plan for your church, you have to take some time to think about your philosophy of worship.

Philosophy, as Cicero said in the first century BC, is simply the love of wisdom. I would also add "love of study" to Cicero's definition. So, philosophy is the love of study and wisdom. In our context, it's the why behind how we structure and run our services. Philosophy, as it relates to worship, is not an ephemeral examination of human interaction with God within the context of the church; it's not your style, though it will help you determine your style. It is a wisdom-driven examination of why you do church the way you do. It's important that you take the time to ask yourself why and then answer your own question. Ultimately, your philosophy of worship will define, motivate, and serve as a measure for your worship services. You can't measure what you can't define, and you can't manage what you can't measure.

> *Ultimately, your philosophy of worship will define, motivate, and serve as a measure for your worship services.*

Your current philosophy of worship is likely one you've fallen into by default—one you were handed by leaders before you, or one you've settled into without much intentional thought. The best way to get an idea of your current philosophy of worship and to determine your ideal philosophy is to play a little word game. Grab some key staff members and get their insight here too. While this is a simple exercise, it is not necessarily easy. But it will be very informative.

On the lines below, write five words that describe your current worship services. Be brave with your answers. Think about what people in your church would say if you were to ask them to describe your services. Honesty is key. If you think your people would call your services boring or long, write those things down. Face your current reality. You can't get where you want to go without first acknowledging where you are.

1. _____

2. _____

3. _____

4. _____

5. _____

The next part of the exercise is more fun. Take a minute to jot down five words you *wish* described your worship services. Here are a few to help you get started:

engaging	inspiring	life-changing	inviting
relevant	passionate	biblical	authentic
God-glorifying	fun	energizing	strong

Philosopher Ludwig Wittgenstein once said, "The limits of your words are the limits of your world." Don't limit yourself or God's dream for your worship. Imagine your church at its best.

Think outside the box. What words would you like to describe your services? Feel free to borrow from the suggestions above.

1. _____
2. _____
3. _____
4. _____
5. _____

Based on the ten words you've written, how big is the chasm between your current worship services and your ideal worship services? How do you cross that divide? If you want to have services that can be described in the way you've just imagined, the first step is to clearly define the philosophy of worship that will get you there. Start by examining the why behind your current state of affairs, and then set about determining a philosophy that will take you and your church to the heights of influence God intends. (You can download a free copy of The Journey's philosophy of worship at www.ChurchLeaderInsights.com/Engage.)

> *Molding the worship planning system to our church's vision and structure without losing the integrity of either the system or our own identity was easy. Everything we do is now run through this system. We are growing closer together as a cohesive unit, aiming for the same goals and celebrating the same successes. I think I may have read about another church somewhere that experienced a similar situation: "And they were all in one place, in one accord." Imagine that. It really is possible!*

> Keith Kannenberg, Lead Pastor
> Blackwelder Park Baptist Church,
> Kannapolis, North Carolina

2

worship

Seven Principles of Life-Transforming Worship

Philosophy is not a theory but an activity.

Ludwig Wittgenstein

Therefore, I urge you, brothers and sisters, in view of God's mercy, to offer your bodies as a living sacrifice, holy and pleasing to God—this is your true and proper worship. Do not conform to the pattern of this world, but be transformed by the renewing of your mind. Then you will be able to test and approve what God's will is—his good, pleasing and perfect will.

Romans 12:1–2 NIV

Congratulations! By simply being willing to step back and ask yourself why you do things the way you do, you have taken a giant leap toward creating more effective worship services. Plus, by daring to envision that your services could be better than they currently are, you are choosing to believe God has something more in store for you and your church. You've acknowledged you could be called to cooperate with God at an even higher level—to partner more intentionally with him in drawing people to himself.

Your next step is to begin building the framework for your new philosophy of worship. At The Journey, we have established seven principles of life-changing worship, built around the acrostic WORSHIP. These seven principles work together to define our philosophy of worship; they are the core values for how we do worship planning. Not to mention, they are also constant, action-oriented reminders that protect us from settling into a status quo.

As you read through these seven principles, allow them to stoke your own creative fire. You don't have to build your philosophy of worship around the same principles, but you do need to establish values that define and anchor your philosophy. Identify what works for you and your church, take what you need from our philosophy, and fill in the gaps to create your own.

WORSHIP

Work as a Team

I grew up in the early days of the internet. In my teenage years, I actually created and sold a small computer business. Before I met Jesus, I thought this kind of entrepreneurship was going to be my path in life. During those days, one of my heroes was Andy Grove, the former chairman of Intel. I once heard Andy say something that stuck with me as I matured and left the business world for ministry: "None of us is as smart as all of us." He couldn't have been more right. You can't underestimate the power of synergy—especially in your worship planning.

As the lead teaching pastor or the worship pastor in your church, you are ultimately responsible for the worship planning, but that doesn't mean you have all the wisdom or that you are capable of doing things on your own. The idea of being able to create life-changing worship services alone is a fallacy. None of us is as smart as all of us. God put a team of staff and volunteers around you for a reason. He wants you to tap into the stores of resources they have to offer as you plan your teaching and worship.

Many teaching pastors I've worked with over the years don't buy into this idea. They see message planning as something they are supposed to do alone in their office, something that is strictly between them and God. End of story. Now don't get me wrong. Your independent study and prayer time are critical to your message preparation. They are the genesis, if you will. God has given you authority and ultimate responsibility for connecting with him concerning what he wants you to translate to your people. But at the same time, it's not all about you. You have to acknowledge that God speaks to many other people on your team who can help expand your teaching exponentially. The same principle applies to the music and artistic elements in your service. Don't be afraid to let other people speak into your area of expertise and offer ideas, illustrations, and different points of view. Your message, worship, and outreach will be stronger because of it. Never limit the sources of God's inspiration.

You've probably heard the acrostic for TEAM: together everyone achieves more. Cliché though it is, it's spot-on. I have a friend who put a slightly different spin on things by changing the last word to *miracles*. Together everyone achieves miracles. That's true at The Journey, and it will be true in your church if you are willing to invite other people into your planning process. As Pat MacMillan wrote in his great work on leadership, *The Performance Factor*, "Leadership today requires leaders who are able to tap into the resources of the group—leaders who can release the initiative and leadership in everyone."[1] As you learn to become that kind of leader, the previously untapped potential of your team will help take your worship planning to a whole new level. Teamwork makes the dream work.

Outline Your Preaching Calendar

As we like to say around our offices, the message drives the day. Likewise, in a strong worship planning system, the upcoming messages and series drive every other element of your planning. So outlining your preaching calendar well in advance is critical. Otherwise, you cripple the other aspects of your worship planning. The only way to have a worship planning system that produces the kind of services you want is to commit to knowing in advance what you are preaching and passing that information to the rest of your team.

Why is advanced planning so important? Creativity doesn't happen under the gun. You can't throw together a life-transforming, synergistic service at the last minute, as I'm sure you've learned the hard way. We certainly have! Rather than limiting your church's potential by always being a step behind, make a decision to outline your preaching a year in advance. That will provide the foundational information that you and your team need to plan all the other service elements properly.

When your staff and volunteers know what's coming down the pike, they can do their part to create worship services that resonate with people. Advanced planning gives both you and your team time to prepare effectively for each and every Sunday.

We will break down exactly how to plan a one-year preaching calendar in part 2. For now, spend some time chewing on the proverb, "Good planning and hard work lead to prosperity, but hasty shortcuts lead to poverty" (Prov. 21:5). If you want your worship services to prosper, good planning—and the hard work that good planning entails—is key. Your calendar sets the stage for every other area of your worship planning potential. (You can download a free copy of The Journey's most current preaching calendar at www.ChurchLeaderInsights.com/Engage.)

Repentance Is the Goal of Worship

Repentance is the ultimate goal of worship, which makes it the number one priority of our worship planning system (see Isaiah 6 for additional study on how repentance follows true worship). Everything we do is designed to call people to repentance. That said, I rarely use the word *repentance* in a message. *Metanoia* is the Greek word commonly translated as "repentance," but it literally means "changed thinking." So I talk about truth that leads to change; I talk about selecting a different option; I talk about taking a divergent path—all with the goal of leading people to repentance, which is a change of thinking and/or a turning from sin.

Many church leaders have the impression that weepy people falling on their faces at the altar is the only real evidence of repentance. While repentance does often take the form of a strong emotional response, it can also be seen in much smaller

35

moments of realization. Repentance is any recognition of sin that leads to an alignment with God's plan and purposes. Here's my favorite working definition of repentance: repentance is a willful, personal response to the continuing call to follow Christ that leads to a change in outlook, action, and obedience.

Teaching pastors must remember that intellectual knowledge is just the beginning of transformation. There must also be a clear call to repentance and, most importantly, the congealing inspiration of God. I don't ever want people to walk out of church and simply think, "Huh. I learned something today." Instead, I want them to think, "I want to live out what I just learned." Information plus inspiration plus action leads to transformation. God provides the inspiration; we provide the information and the call to action.

> *Repentance is the deepest kind of worship.*

None of us is in the business of creating transformation in people. God is the only one who can do that. Our job is to create an environment where the transformation can happen and intentionally invite our listeners into God's truth. If people aren't seeing their lives transformed by the reality of Jesus Christ, we may not be doing our part to make sure the worship service is having the effect God wants it to have. People should be more like Jesus when they walk out of our churches than when they walked in, and every aspect of our services should be created with that goal in mind. Repentance is the deepest kind of worship.

Sunday Matters

The hour or so that you have with your people during each worship service is phenomenally important. Every. Single. Week.

You can never let a Sunday slide. Every Sunday matters. One of the most basic requirements for being a teaching pastor or a worship leader is that you love Sundays. God has entrusted you with people who will walk through your doors on Sunday morning (or whenever you have your services) looking for a connection to him. You are responsible for upholding your end of the deal and creating the best worship service possible.

The hour or so that you have with your people during each worship service is phenomenally important.

Since Sundays are so important, at The Journey we have decided never to leave anything associated with the Sunday service to chance. In fact, we have a rule called the Thursday midnight rule. By midnight on Thursday, we are totally prepared for Sunday—down to every last detail. We don't want to run into any unexpected problems on Sunday morning. By Thursday at midnight, everything is printed and ready to go, so we don't run the risk of last-minute printing issues. All the equipment for the worship team is packed and loaded in the van to take to our portable venue. We've learned not to wait to do anything that can be done in advance—even if it is just bringing an extra microphone wire to the stage. Leave nothing to chance. God honors preparedness. (To learn more about the Thursday midnight rule, download the free audio resource at www. ChurchLeaderInsights.com/Engage.)

Over the years, the only staff members I've had to let go—and there haven't been many—were ones who didn't love Sundays. Sunday is our game day. It is the reason we do what we do as church leaders. It's what we spend the week preparing for. We can never afford to phone it in. We can never afford to tweak last week's worship order and go another round. We are called to a higher purpose. This Sunday could be the Sunday someone who hasn't been to church in thirty years walks through your doors. This Sunday could be the Sunday God wants to use you to work a miracle in someone's life. This Sunday could be the Sunday someone's eternity changes. You have been given the awesome responsibility of cooperating with God in bringing his purposes to pass. Be fully engaged and ready to work every week. Sunday matters!

Honor God through Excellence

We are a reflection of God's character on this earth. God isn't sloppy or ill prepared; he's excellent. And excellence on our part honors him. Where you and I get into trouble is in thinking that excellence is the same as perfection. It isn't. We will never be perfect this side of heaven. But that doesn't mean we can't reflect our Father's perfection by being excellent in all we do. As Nancy Beach says in her book *An Hour on Sunday*, excellence is simply doing the best we can with what God has given us.

Remember Jesus's words in Matthew 25:23: "The master said, 'Well done, my good and faithful servant. You have been faithful in handling this small amount, so now I will give you many more responsibilities. Let's celebrate together!'" Your current congregation—no matter its size—is the "small amount" you've been given. As you are faithful in handling this small amount according to God's purposes and reflecting his excellence, he will be able to trust you with even greater responsibilities.

Instead of continually praying for more, prove your faithfulness by doing the very best you can with what you've already been given. If your worship team is just you and a guitar, be excellent in that position. When the timing is right, God will bring you more musicians. If your congregation is only a handful of people, be faithful to shepherd them with excellence and God will expand your territory. You and I honor God when we commit to doing the very best we can with what we have. To offer God anything less is a sin. You don't have to get it right every time, but you do have to give it everything you've got.

> *You and I honor God when we commit to doing the very best we can with what we have.*

Invite People to Take Next Steps

What happens in your services is of no use to your people if they don't walk away with a clear understanding of how to incorporate the teaching and worship into their lives. That's why it is so important to begin your worship planning with the end in mind. As Stephen Covey writes in his great work, *The Seven Habits of Highly Effective People*, "To begin with the end in mind means to start with a clear understanding of your destination. It means to know where you are going so that you better understand where you are now and so that the steps you take are always in the right direction."[2] In other words, determine how you are going to land your message before you even begin.

At The Journey, we do this by asking and prayerfully answering these three questions in the early stages of our planning for each service:

1. What do we want people to *know* when they leave?
2. What do we want people to *feel* when they leave?
3. What do we want people to *do* when they leave?

What do you want people to have learned when you are finished? What do you want them to be feeling? And, most importantly, what action steps do you want them to take to integrate the themes of the service into their lives? Thinking through the "know, feel, do" as you craft your worship services is the best way to define where you are going and to get there more effectively. If you don't answer these questions in advance, you run the very real risk of wasting both your time and your congregation's.

Let's take a look at how the "know, feel, do" plays out in practice. Say, for example, I am planning a message on generosity. At the outset of my planning, I would start thinking through the "know, feel, do" questions in relation to generosity. I may decide that my big theme for the day will be: "Your life will ultimately be defined by one of two G words: greed (closed-handed living) or generosity (open-handed living)." That's what I want my people to know. Then I want them to feel the power of generosity, so I would think through how to invoke that feeling. But keep in mind, the feeling is only important if it motivates them to take an action. So, ultimately, I am concerned with the do. I want them to be motivated to actually give. I want them to give of their time through serving or to give of their money to our giving campaign or to the needy in our city. I want them to take an action step that connects what they're hearing with how they live when they step outside the church doors.

Never end a service without giving people specific next steps they can take in response to God's teaching. Scripture is clear on this point: "But don't just listen to God's word. You must do what it says. Otherwise, you are only fooling yourselves" (James 1:22). We don't have a lack of knowledge in American churches. We don't even have a lack of experience or feeling.

What we have is a lack of action. People simply don't do what the Bible says they should do. By asking the "know, feel, do" questions as you plan your worship, you can help your people know what God wants them to know and feel what God wants them to feel, with the ultimate goal of helping them do what God wants them to do. Otherwise we are only helping them fool themselves. (To learn more about how The Journey uses next steps in the worship service, see my earlier book *Fusion: Turning First-Time Guests into Fully-Engaged Members of Your Church* [Regal, 2007] or download the free Journey Connection Card at www.ChurchLeaderInsights.com/Engage.)

> *The thing that has helped us the most is asking the three questions: What do we want people to know? What do we want people to feel? What do we want people to do? Working through these questions helps us set the tone of each service we are planning. We choose music, testimonies, videos, and other elements based on how our answers to these questions direct us. Not to mention, asking these three questions each week has helped me in my sermon preparation. Knowing what we want our people to know and feel helps me narrow my message down to one main idea. Knowing what we want them to do helps me formulate the next steps we will be asking our people to take.*
>
> Jay Richardson, Senior Pastor
> Highland Colony Baptist Church, Ridgeland, Mississippi

Planning Honors God

Have you ever come across church leaders who confuse laziness with godliness? These are the people who argue that they don't like to put too much planning into their services because they want to leave room for God's Spirit to work. Such thinking is not an invitation for the Holy Spirit to work but rather a simple excuse for laziness. Any pastor can pick up his Bible on Saturday night, read through a few verses, and then get up and talk for thirty minutes on Sunday. Any worship pastor can come up with three or four songs the day before the service. Contrary to their popular belief, pastors and worship pastors who operate this way are not being more spiritual; they are actually dishonoring God. Remember our call to excellence? It's impossible to be excellent without prayerful preparation.

Teaching pastors and worship pastors who choose to adopt this mind-set have always reminded me of students who wait until the last minute to study for a test they've known was coming for weeks. They cram for a few minutes the night before the big day and then sit down in front of the test, pencil in hand, and say, "God, please help me," before diving in. God is not going to give such ill-prepared students the answers. But if they had taken time to prepare for the test—to live up to their responsibility as students—then God would certainly help them stay calm, synthesize all the information, and do their best.

The Holy Spirit is perfectly capable of giving you insight and direction for your upcoming worship services as you honor God through preparation. He can move and inspire you just as powerfully two Thursdays before your message as he can the night before or the morning of—and you'll be in a better position to hear from him. In fact, I would argue that you aren't able to hear from God nearly as effectively when you wait until the last minute to plan.

Consider this scenario. Say you and I are walking down a busy New York City sidewalk during rush hour. Imagine the chaos around us—people brushing by talking loudly on their cell phones, jackhammers breaking into the concrete streets, sirens whirring from every direction, horns honking, people calling out to their friends, groups of kids laughing, music spilling out of open-air shops . . . You get the picture. What if I had something really important I needed to tell you, and that moment was my only opportunity? I may lean in and try to speak into your ear, but you would be so distracted by the commotion around us that you wouldn't be able to focus on what I was saying. Hearing me clearly would be nearly impossible.

That's how it is when you wait until the last minute to plan your services. Of course God wants to speak to you then—he always wants to speak to you—but there is so much chaos as you try to get ready for the upcoming weekend that you have a difficult time hearing him clearly. Last-minute distractions keep you from being able to focus on his heart. But if you sought him in advance, you will be attuned to his direction for your Sunday service well before the week-of details try to steal your attention. Not to mention, if God has anything additional he'd like to tell you at the last minute, you will have the margin to make changes—changes that may be significant to the power of your service but that you never would have gotten to if you hadn't already done the work of planning.

Planning prepares you for God to move and paves the way for excellence. Planning is also extremely biblical. Again, Proverbs 21:5 says, "Good planning and hard work lead to prosperity, but hasty shortcuts lead to poverty." Proverbs 21:31 follows that up with, "The horse is prepared for the day of battle, but the victory belongs to the LORD." At the end of the day, God will bring the victory. I can rest in the knowledge that God will do what only he can do. But, as the proverb suggests, someone has to get the horse ready for the battle; that's our job. Winging it is not an option in kingdom work. Of course, we acknowledge that the ultimate result of our efforts lies in God's hands, but we are in no way to use that as an excuse to shirk our God-given responsibility.

There's an old joke about a religious devotee who visited the same saint's statue every day and prayed, "Dear saint, please, please, please help me win the lottery." One day, as the man was praying this prayer for the umpteenth time, the frustrated statue came to life and said, "My son, please, please, please buy a ticket!" This tongue-in-cheek joke underscores a reality we all need to remember: no matter what we are expecting from God, he wants us to hold up our end of the bargain. God doesn't reward our laziness; he works through our preparation.

(To learn more about these seven values and how to craft your own, see the "Planning Worship Services for Life Transformation" resource at www.ChurchLeaderInsights.com/Engage.)

Our church is a ninety-four-year-old Pentecostal church, and we believe very much in allowing the Spirit to move during the service. We used to go into our Sunday services with very little planned, and the lack of planning was apparent. We would say we wanted to let the Spirit move, but the reality was that we were trying to do things on the fly. We'd call someone out of the congregation to make an announcement at a moment's notice. The head usher would tap someone on the shoulder on his way up the aisle to help collect the offering. Each week, after the service, we would realize many things we had missed. Ultimately, we realized that we weren't being effective. Even though we have been around for almost a century, we never want to stop learn-

ing. With the worship planning system, we learned that the Holy Spirit is very capable of planning in advance. If we get to Sunday and realize that God is doing something different, then okay. But we have learned to do our part and plan along with the Holy Spirit. And God is now moving in our services in an even greater way. We are seeing more lives changed.

Terry Drost, Lead Pastor
Peckville Assembly of God, Blakely, Pennsylvania

Homework

Now that you know what defines our philosophy of worship at The Journey, I have some homework for you. Before you go any further in your study of implementing an effective worship planning system, I want you to take the time to think through the following six questions. These questions will combine with what you have just learned about the seven principles of life-transforming worship, and with your own prayer and study, to give you the tools you need to develop your philosophy of worship. (For a free download of the philosophy of worship questionnaire to use with your team, visit www.ChurchLeader Insights.com/Engage.)

1. Why do you hold services each Sunday? _____

_____

_____

_____

_____

_____

_____

2. What is the role of the Sunday services in the life of your people? _____

_____

_____

_____

_____

_____

_____

_____

3. How do you measure the effectiveness of your Sunday services? _____

_____

_____

_____

_____

_____

_____

4. If your church stopped holding Sunday services, would anyone other than the current attenders even notice?

_____

_____

_____

_____

_____

_____

_____

5. Are you excited about the Sunday services at your church?

_____

_____

_____

_____

_____

_____

_____

_____

6. When was the last time you did a theological study of worship? _____

_____

_____

_____

_____

_____

_____

_____

Once you have nailed down the philosophy of worship for your church, post your core values in a place where you'll see them often. Allow them to continually remind you of the strategic partnership you've been invited into by God to create the atmosphere and opportunity for him to transform lives.

preaching
calendar

3

wanted

Radically Transformed Lives

The test of a preacher is that his congregation goes away saying
not, "What a lovely sermon!" but "I will do something."

Billy Graham

I brought glory to you here on earth by completing the work
you gave me to do.

John 17:4

Does your congregation remember what you preached
last Sunday? How about the Sunday before that? I
don't want to burst your bubble, but numerous studies over
the years have shown that people forget the majority of the
information they hear from a communicator within twenty-
four hours. Chances are, every message you work so hard to

prepare and then deliver with such eloquence is all but forgotten by the time your listeners have their Monday morning cup of coffee. But you don't have time to worry about the teaching that has faded into oblivion; you are too busy preparing for next week.

I'm sure you've experienced the frustration of feeling like your people aren't hearing what you are trying so desperately to get across to them. Even if it seems like you've connected with them during the service itself, so often their actions in the days and weeks after prove they didn't integrate the truths into their lives. Seeing your efforts result in a lack of life change time and time again can be discouraging, to say the least. If you are like me, you've probably asked yourself at one time or another, "Why do I even preach at all? What's the point?"

God's plan from the beginning of time has been to call people to himself and then to grow them to be more like his Son. He accomplishes this in many ways—through life circumstances, through his Word, through prayer, through small groups . . . The list goes on and on. But one of the primary tools God wants to use to develop his people is the teaching of those of us who have been called to the pulpit. God's plan for redemption includes using you and me to help people meet Jesus and then become more like him every day. We do what we do week in and week out to cooperate with God in creating transformed lives. Life change is the goal.

Notice what the goal is not. The goal is not to share information. The goal is not to increase your listeners' knowledge of biblical history as an end unto itself. The goal is not to win the accolades of the elders or get high fives from your family around the lunch table. All of those things may be nice side effects of preaching well, but they are certainly not the priority. You stand in front of your people on Sunday mornings for one reason and one reason only: to connect God's truth to real life in a way that leads to radical transformation.

So if your goal is to connect with people in a way that leads to life change, but most people forget the majority of what they hear within hours, there's a gap that needs to be addressed. When people aren't internalizing what they experience in your services, their lives won't change. The question then becomes, how do you preach in a way that truly engages people and leads to radically transformed lives? The first step is to figure out how well you are doing right now. Are you preaching to share information or to foster transformation? Is your teaching on God's truth making it into your people's hearts, or is it simply taking flight into the annals of preaching history? You need a way to measure your current level of effectiveness.

> *You stand in front of your people on Sunday mornings for one reason and one reason only: to connect God's truth to real life in a way that leads to radical transformation.*

At The Journey, we are always inventing ways to measure things. We believe you can't manage what you can't measure. To measure the effectiveness of our services, we came up with an analogy based on America's favorite pastime: baseball. Using a baseball diamond to frame our thinking, we began asking ourselves, "How do we move people around the bases?" or rather, "How do we move people to the next step in their spiritual growth?"

In baseball, the players' ultimate goal is to garner a high number of RBIs—runs batted in. By mastering the essentials of effective play—running, hitting, catching, and throwing—teams move people around the bases. Their singular objective is to move each runner to first, then second, then third base, and finally back to home plate, where he can dramatically slide in for a score, putting another RBI on the board.

In our analogy, we aren't interested in RBIs but in RTLs—radically transformed lives. We discovered that if we could master the essentials of moving people to the next step in their spiritual growth—moving them around the bases, so to speak—then their lives would be radically transformed as they become more and more like Jesus. By establishing this simple measurement, we were able to begin tracking the effectiveness of what we were doing on Sunday mornings. Radically transformed lives became both our goal and our gauge. (To learn more about radically transformed lives, download the free "How to Preach for Radically Transformed Lives" article at www.ChurchLeaderInsights .com/Engage.)

Every baseball team needs strong hitters, fast runners, and adept catchers if they are going to win games. Likewise, your church needs three types of "players" if you hope to cooperate with God in fostering radically transformed lives: unbelievers, new believers, and maturing believers.

Rooting for the Home Team

Unbelievers: The unbelievers in your service are the batters on deck. Without them, your church can't be healthy, and RTLs simply won't happen at the rate God intends. Imagine a baseball team with no batters lined up. The game would wither pretty quickly. As a rule of thumb, you should average at least five unchurched first-time guests for every one hundred regular attenders in each of your services. A ratio less than this will result in disease. (For detailed teaching on how to grow the number of first-time guests in your church, see my book *Ignite: How to Spark Immediate Growth in Your Church* [Baker, 2009], or visit www.ChurchLeaderInsights .com/Engage.)

New believers: Once unbelievers come through your doors, you have the monumental opportunity and responsibility to introduce them to Jesus. You need to create an environment where your guests are comfortable and feel welcome so they'll continue to come back to your church and learn more about God. (For more on turning first-time guests into members, see *Fusion: Turning First-Time Guests into Fully-Engaged Members of Your Church* [Regal, 2007], or visit www.ChurchLeader Insights.com/Engage.) As a teaching pastor, you should be particularly effective at communicating the truth of the gospel to unbelievers. You are responsible for introducing them to the person of Jesus in the most relevant, empathetic way possible. In terms of our analogy, entering into a relationship with Jesus gets people on base.

Maturing believers: As the old saying goes, "God accepts you just as you are, but he doesn't want to leave you that way." Both new and more mature believers need to be continually challenged to take the next step in their spiritual growth—whatever next step will help them become more fully developing followers of Jesus. Action steps move your people around the bases and ultimately add up to RTLs. (To learn more about moving people around the bases, beginning with membership, see the "Maximizing Membership" resource at www.ChurchLeaderInsights.com/ Engage.)

Pastor Tim steps out of the rain and into the busy diner. As he shakes out his umbrella, he looks around for his friend David. He and David have been meeting for breakfast the second Tuesday of every month for at least two years. David is about eight years younger and just starting out as the lead teaching pastor in a church across town. Tim considers himself something of a mentor to his friend—at least, he hopes God is using him that way. Tim spots David in the corner booth talking to the server.

Sliding in across from David and shucking off his wet jacket, Tim says, "Morning! Man, it's blowing up a storm out there."

"Hey, Tim," David answers. "Sure is. Makes this place all the more inviting. I just ordered the first round of coffee."

After catching up on each other's family news and talking a little about the upcoming baseball season, they settle into shoptalk.

"Speaking of baseball, I've been thinking about that analogy you were describing to me last month," David says. "You know, it really makes sense. You made me realize that the pastor at my church growing up preached to share information. He was such a knowledgeable man. He could exegete any passage of Scripture blindfolded and standing on his head, but no one ever seemed to get much out of his messages. Now I understand why. He wasn't preaching for transformation."

"Yeah, David, that's happening in churches all over the world. We have so much knowledge these days, so much information, but not enough life change," Tim replies.

"How do you get around that?" asks David. "I mean, how do you really make your teaching connect so that people are taking their next step toward growth? Knowing how to measure RTLs is great, but how do you actually move people around the bases?"

"Planning."

"Planning?"

"Yep," Tim answers. "Planning. Preaching that radically transforms lives requires advance planning. You have to get to the point where you plan your preaching calendar an entire year out. When you do, you have the freedom and the opportunity to cooperate with the Holy Spirit in creating messages and entire services that really allow for transformation."

"That seems like a pretty daunting task," David says.

"It's a little intimidating at first, but actually, planning in advance will cause such drastic changes in the life of your church that you'll wonder how you ever operated without doing it. Not to mention, it will take a ton of pressure off your shoulders week to week."

"Huh." David pushes the last few bites of his pancakes around on his plate, thinking about what Tim is saying.

"David, when I first started out in ministry, a good friend of mine told me something I've never forgotten. He said, 'Tim, someone pays the price for the sermon. Either the preacher pays the price of planning, or the people pay the price of wasted time.'" Tim takes a bite of his toast and signals the server for more coffee.

Plan Your Preaching

Remember the P of our WORSHIP philosophy? Planning honors God. Planning in advance is the only way you and I will be able to create life-changing worship services that reflect God's excellence and allow him to work to the fullest degree. And here's the key, teaching pastor: your preaching calendar sets the stage for your church's entire planning system. Your preaching calendar is the foundation; it's the backbone that supports every other area of your worship planning. When you commit to outlining your preaching in advance, you give yourself, your team, and ultimately your congregation a gift—the gift of teaching and worship that creates life change. Without advance planning, you run the risk of simply sharing information that will be forgotten at the final amen.

Think back to the "know, feel, do" exercise we discussed in the last chapter. Part of planning your preaching is being able to put yourself in the shoes of the people who sit in front of you on a Sunday morning. I like to ask myself, "If I were preaching to me, would I know what I was supposed to do after hearing the message?" By thinking through the "know, feel, do" points, you can ensure that you aren't just planning to teach for knowledge but for life application.

Before we jump into the nuts and bolts of putting together your preaching calendar, I want you to understand beyond a shadow of a doubt why this kind of planning is critical. Here are the five top reasons to plan your preaching.

Planning Provides Balance

The five primary purposes of the church are worship, fellowship, discipleship, evangelism, and service. Without an intentional plan to balance these five purposes in your preaching, you will overemphasize the purpose that most reflects your own passion and gifting. If you are most passionate about evangelism, every time you sit down to prepare a message, you are going to drift toward evangelism. If you are most passionate about stewardship, too much of your teaching will end up in that territory. That's why every sermon series and every stand-alone message you and I preach should be intentionally centered on one of the five purposes. A preaching calendar allows you to do just that. It will keep you on track, helping you to balance your year around all the purposes that your people need to embrace.

The vast majority of pastors I work with want to know the answer to the question, how do I get my church to grow? But that's not the right question to ask. The right question is, how do I get my church healthy? Healthy organisms grow naturally. Balance in your church leads to health. If there is no balance— and therefore no health—your church won't grow, nor will your people. As teaching pastors, we need to take Paul's words from Acts 20:27 to heart: "For I didn't shrink from declaring all that God wants you to know." Don't stunt your RTLs by focusing too intently on one purpose. Let your preaching calendar be the tool that will help you declare to your people all that God wants them to know.

I learned early on as a pastor about my tendency to preach in circles, to gravitate back to my favorite topics. The worship planning system helped me not only to be able to plan as much as a year in advance (a tremendous blessing regarding stress) but also to offer my people a more balanced diet from God's Word.

Mike Russell, Pastor
Oak Hill Baptist Church, Meridian, Mississippi

Planning Produces Greater Creativity

God is creative. Just consider all the animals he has uniquely designed. Would you have come up with a duck-billed platypus or an emperor tamarin? Appreciating the power of creativity, God allows you and me the space to be creative in bringing people into a greater knowledge of him. But creativity doesn't happen under the gun. Sure, you may be able to pull together a half-decent message and music for an upcoming service at the last minute, but you won't be able to create graphics, pull movie clips, or write and rehearse a drama. However, when you know what you are teaching in advance, you give yourself and your team the opportunity to plan creative, synergistic services that will engage hearts and minds.

Have you ever wished that your worship pastor were more creative? His lack of creativity is most likely a direct result of your lack of planning. Think of it this way: your preaching calendar defines the borders of the canvas on which your service is going to be created. Great creativity always happens within a defined space. Painters need a canvas. Sketch artists need paper. Actors need a stage. And your worship pastor needs to know in advance what you are going to be preaching in order to do his job to the best of his ability. You can't ask your worship pastor and your creative team to be more creative if you aren't doing your part to provide the tools necessary to that creativity. You have to bind the canvas before the creative work can begin. (To learn more about The Journey's nine core values for music planning, plus how your worship leader can create a music plan in advance and lead a music planning meeting, check out the "Leading with Authority in Rehearsal" resource at www .ChurchLeaderInsights.com/Engage.)

Planning Provides Greater Depth

I have a friend who says that preparing a good sermon is like preparing a good soup. After you add all the ingredients, you have to let it simmer for a while. Deep preaching grows out of advance study and preparation—the kind of advance study and preparation that is possible only with a preaching calendar. When you know in advance what topics and Scripture passages you are tackling, you have time to let your thoughts marinate. You can season them with tidbits of life experience that you run into during the weeks leading up to your message. You give the Holy Spirit plenty of room to thicken things to his liking. Conversely, a lack of preparation leads to both lack of depth and lack of resulting action. No matter how many Greek and Hebrew words you throw into your teaching, it won't result in radically changed lives unless you give it the full preparation time it needs. Weak soup simply can't nourish as effectively.

Planning Prompts the Holy Spirit to Work Both in Advance and the Day Of

I'm always surprised when I hear comments like "I don't want to plan ahead because I don't want to box God in." First of all, neither you nor I are capable of boxing God in. Second, if you believe that God is omniscient—and I assume you do—then planning ahead makes perfect sense. He already knows what's going to happen in your life, your people's lives, and the world over the next year. You don't. If you are seeking his voice and direction as you put together your calendar, you will be following his lead into territory that he has the inside track on. God encourages planning throughout his Word. There is no plausible excuse for not agreeing with him, for not giving his work the time and attention it deserves. I have just one note of warning: be prepared for him to show up in mind-boggling ways.

Early in the history of The Journey, we were led to do a series on the Lord's Prayer. Months ahead of time, we gave the series the working title "The Path to Peace in the City." For some reason, we could never shake that working title. Even though I didn't love it, it stuck. Well, as God would have it, "The Path to Peace in the City" kicked off the Sunday after our country went to war with Iraq. Everyone I spoke to that Sunday asked me how we were able to plan such an applicable message so quickly. Many people were at church that day because they had friends who had been deployed or they had lost a loved one in the 9/11 attacks, and they were astonished by the series' timeliness. So were we!

God had led us to put that message series, with that exact title, in that precise slot on the calendar almost a year before. He knew what the future held. All we did was cooperate with his purposes by planning. We have seen God's timing play out in phenomenal ways like this many times over.

One more thing: advance planning in no way negates our dependence on the Holy Spirit on Sunday. I am still utterly dependent on him to show up each week. Often he'll reveal illustrations, tweaks, or additions the night before or the day of a message. I have the flexibility to add in those things. But when the Holy Spirit is working on Sunday mornings, he is working in a specific environment that he has prompted me to design months in advance. It doesn't get much cooler than that. When you teach exactly what God wants you to teach on the exact Sunday he wants you to teach it, in an environment he has driven you to create, lives will be changed. People won't walk away forgetting what they've heard.

Planning Produces Maximum Results

As you've seen already, planning has the potential to produce the best possible results in every area of your church. Planning your preaching calendar in advance lays the foundation for creating powerful, engaging worship experiences. As you plan, you have the ability to create entire services that will resonate with your listeners long after you've settled in for your Sunday afternoon nap. You will have the freedom to structure your entire worship planning system in a way that breeds and celebrates lives that are being radically transformed by God. Why would you pass up the opportunity to cooperate with God in such a significant way? This calling is not about sharing information on a Sunday morning; it's about life transformation. What are your people doing on Thursday as a result of what they experienced on Sunday? That's the real test. Planning in advance leads to life-changing results.

In *Communicating for a Change*, Andy Stanley writes, "While we must pay attention to and work to improve our performance on the platform, there is something else to consider as well. Namely, the outcome. What people do as a result of what we say. The audience's willingness to act on what they have heard. Life change."[3] When you fully understand that your weekly goal is to connect God's truth to real life in a way that leads to radical transformation, that reality changes the way you operate. You will commit to crafting your services from a new perspective—a perspective that pushes you to create environments that are conduits of true life change. Those environments begin with your preaching calendar. So let's get on to the details of putting it together.

The preaching calendar is a revolutionary application of "doing church." Before it, I had tried everything I could think of with

63

my preaching—book preaching, lectionary preaching, "Spirit-led" preaching (randomly picking things). I was faithful to the gospel, I believe, but ultimately underperforming. The effectiveness of the preaching calendar is that it is not *a new program, a new method, or the latest and greatest thing for the church to try. I've started and forgotten dozens of those. Simply put, the systematic approach behind the preaching calendar allowed me to finally see the "big picture" for the direction of the church and how all the pieces fit together. It is like a puzzle. I had the pieces, but I finally found the box with the picture on it, so I know what the pieces are supposed to form. This is the start of a transformation in our church.*

Reverend Peter Hofstra
First Presbyterian Church, Perth Amboy, New Jersey

4

laying a solid foundation

How to Plan Your Preaching

It pays to plan ahead. It wasn't raining when Noah built the ark.

Anonymous

So teach us to number our days,
    that we may present to You a heart of wisdom.

Psalm 90:12 NASB

Have you ever tried to persuade your son or daughter to do algebra in the middle of the summer? Have you ever given someone a Christmas present in September? How about this one: have you ever tried to pull out the barbeque and grill some dinner in a foot of snow? You *could* do all three of these things, and maybe you have on occasion, but they don't make much sense. To kids, summer is for fun and sun; they don't want to think about anything academic. Sure, you can give presents anytime of year, but it would feel a little odd to pull out a green and red package while the sun is shining brightly through golden fall leaves. As for grilling in the snow, well, that just doesn't make any sense, does it?

The counterintuitiveness of these three propositions is obvious. We can easily see that each one contradicts the natural rhythm of our lives. Yet in the church, we operate against natural rhythms all the time and then wonder why our services don't engage the people we are trying to influence. If we are willing to become attuned to the way people's lives are inherently structured, we can begin to plan our preaching in a way that takes advantage of the natural ebbs and flows. As we do, we will be able to connect the right messages with the right listeners during the times they'll be most ready to receive them.

The church has always grown the fastest during periods when it has cooperated with, rather than competed against, societal systems. Yet, unfortunately, most of today's churches are in competition mode. Just think about all the countercultural competition we've built into our worldview: the school calendar vs. the church calendar; secular music vs. Christian music; regular television vs. Christian television; mainstream movies vs. Christian movies; contemporary education vs. Christian education.

By creating such a bubble of separation between the believing world and the unbelieving world, we have put ourselves in danger of becoming ineffective. The unchurched may be curious about God and want to learn about his Son, but they stay at arm's length because they are intimidated by our thickly woven

Christian culture. On the other side of the coin, we are unwittingly fostering a generation of believers who can't communicate with non-Christians because they function in an entirely separate reality. They are reverent but not relevant. But that's another conversation altogether.

The church is most efficient at connecting with new believers and growing current ones when it rides the same rails as society's systems rather than building its own set of tracks. In Michael Green's great volume, *Evangelism in the Early Church*, he describes how the earliest Christians fueled the passion of the infant church and won converts in astounding numbers by integrating their transformed lives with the culture and people around them—the people Jesus had come to save and to whom they had been called (as have we).

Referring to these early Christians, including Paul and all the apostles, Green writes, "They made use of all the cultural and intellectual pathways which would facilitate the reception of [their] message. Intensely sensitive to the felt needs of the listeners, the thought world in which they moved, the very language which would strike the clearest note in their minds, their aim nevertheless remained both simple and direct, to introduce others to Jesus Christ."[4]

As modern-day church leaders, many of us are guilty of operating too exclusively in the church world and, by default, neglecting the real world in which our people function. We spend our days, set our schedules, and plan our services with blinders on. We fail to consider the customs and calendar in which everyday people are steeped. One of the best ways we can break out of this self-imposed isolation and begin following the lead of the early church is simply by acknowl-

preaching calendar

edging the ubiquity of the academic calendar as we plan our preaching.

The American education system has taught us to think a certain way. Its nuances structure the year for most families. Even if people don't have children, the rhythm of the school calendar is still ingrained in their psyche from their own years as students. We start fresh in the fall, slow down around Christmas, get back into the swing of things early in the new year, take a break around Easter, and then press on until the summer sun gives us permission to play. The overwhelming majority of Americans operate by these ebbs and flows. If you learn to ride the reality of that ingrained system—taking advantage of the natural stress and release of it to maximize your preaching calendar—you will see more impact, life change, and growth in your church.

Planning Your Preaching Calendar

Keeping the natural flow of the year in mind, let's dive into the details of putting a one-year preaching calendar in place.

Step 1: Examine Your Calendar

No matter what time of year you are beginning this process, the first step is to pull out your calendar and take a comprehensive look at your next twelve months. Go ahead and mark Christmas and Easter as important days. Then as you examine the year ahead, there are three questions you must answer to structure your preaching calendar in a way that cooperates with the innate rhythm of the year. Answering these questions is crucial to creating engaging services and fostering RTLs.

Question 1: At what times of the year is your church best able to reach new, unchurched people?

There are specific times of the year when your church is naturally going to be able to reach more new people. Get your hands on your attendance records over the last two to five years and look for your largest attendance spikes. When does your church see the greatest influx of new attenders? Generally speaking, there are three times of year when churches are most likely to reach the unchurched:

1. February—By early February, people are starting to settle into the new year. They are usually staying close to home after a season of hectic travel and high expense. Not to mention, February is a time of year when people feel a lot of relational strain. These factors work together to make February a high attendance month in most churches.

2. September/October—You should see an influx of new attenders the month after school starts in your area. You won't see them in the week or two after the school year begins; they need three or four weeks to get back into the swing of a regular routine. But once the school year is rolling, people are particularly open to recommitting to church or attending for the first time.

3. Easter Sunday—Easter is the best Sunday of the year to reach new people. More unchurched individuals go to church on Easter Sunday than any other week of the year. Easter gives you a huge opportunity for impact.

Most American churches see a natural boon in attendance during these three times of year. As you look at your records, you may notice a high number of first- and second-time guests during another time of year. If so, make note of it in your calendar.

Question 2: At what times of the year does your church have the highest and steadiest attendance?

In other words, when does your attendance not fluctuate? There are certain times of the year when people are likely to be more consistent in their attendance based on the natural tempo of their calendars. According to your observations and attendance records, when do those periods occur in your church? For many churches, attendance is the steadiest for a stretch during the spring (February to May) and then again for a stretch during the fall (September to November). Taking note of when you maintain momentum will help you set up your calendar purposefully.

Question 3: At what times of the year does your attendance fluctuate the most?

When is your attendance the most unpredictable? When do you see dives? Maybe it's July, because that's when everyone in your town vacations. Maybe it's Thanksgiving weekend. Mark those times down. They will prove important for your planning purposes. (You can download a free copy of The Journey's most current annual preaching calendar at www.ChurchLeader Insights.com/Engage.)

> *We've always had a sense of the best seasons for growth throughout the calendar year, but the worship planning system put our thinking on steroids. Now our planning process involves not just growth seasons but also a specific plan for downtimes. We now see these downtimes as essential seasons of discipleship and*

assimilation. The result has been continued growth during both a difficult time in our economy and a declining population in our community.

Mike Meeks, Lead Pastor
East Lake Church, Chula Vista, California

Step 2: Line Up Message Series with Calendar Flow

After examining your calendar, you should see some definite trends in your attendance. The next step is to begin lining up potential message series with the natural flow of your year. Planning your preaching calendar is ultimately a process of laying several four-to-six-week message series back-to-back over the course of a year. By the time you lay out eight to ten series, your year will be covered. But you can't simply teach whatever series you want to teach whenever you want to teach it. This is not a random process.

Consider placing each message series into one of three categories: an attraction series, a growth series, or a balance series. Each type of series correlates most effectively with specific times of the year. The key to planning your preaching for maximum impact is to layer your attraction, growth, and balance series strategically over the natural attendance patterns of your yearly calendar.

Attraction Series	Growth Series	Balance Series
high felt need	high commitment	important issues
attractive to churched and unchurched	focused on helping attendees become more like Jesus	designed to help believers mature and to inform unbelievers
use when best able to reach new people	use when attendance is high and steady	use when attendance naturally fluctuates

71

The managers of baseball teams are painstakingly intentional about how they set up their batting order. They do it in a way that will ensure the highest possible number of RBIs. As you probably know, in a nine-slot baseball lineup, different batters serve different purposes. The first three batters in the lineup are the best hitters and fastest runners on the team—the guys who can get themselves on base. Batters four to six are the team's power hitters. They hit a lot of home runs, so they are most likely to drive in the guys who are already on base. Hitters seven to nine may not be the strongest batters, but they are usually phenomenal defensive players. They bring balance to the overall team strategy.

In the same way baseball managers carefully structure their lineups, you have a responsibility to position your messages in a way that will give you the best opportunity for inciting life change. If you are intentional in your scheduling—placing your attraction series, growth series, and balance series at the most opportune times of the year—you will make significant strides in producing the maximum number of RTLs for God's glory. Let's look at each type of series in more detail.

Attraction series. An attraction series is comparable to the first three batters in a baseball lineup. This is the type of series that brings new people to your church. That being the case, you should schedule an attraction series during the times of year when you are best able to reach new and unchurched people in your community: February, Easter Sunday, September/October, and other big days in your calendar year, as determined above.

The best attraction series focus on a high felt need topic. Pinpoint an issue that will both intrigue the unchurched and shepherd your current attenders. At The Journey, we do a relationship series every February. Our city and our church are both filled with single and newly married young adults, so sexual issues are a definite felt need. During a February attraction series focused on relationships and sex, we discuss things such as what God says about sex, how to deal with temptation, what the Bible says about purity, and how to safeguard your marriage against adultery. These topics interest our people, draw newcomers to our church, and keep everyone coming back week to week. Though I would enjoy it, a series on propitiation and sanctification probably wouldn't have the same effect—and I would be missing a huge opportunity to take advantage of a time of year when new people are most likely to come to church.

One Easter, we kicked off an attraction series called "Work Matters," which was a study of the book of James. We started on Easter Sunday with a discussion of how the power of the resurrection is tied to everyday life. Then for the next several weeks, we dealt with difficult issues related to the workplace. Why? Because 99 percent of people in New York City are stressed out at work. They are desperate to find meaning in the careers to which they are dedicating their lives. We knew that many of these frustrated people would walk through our doors on Easter Sunday, so we strategically planned a series kickoff that would meet them where they were and give them a reason to return.

Topics related to family life make great attraction series for the month after school begins. If you can offer unchurched couples truth about raising a healthy family or having a healthy marriage, you will be connecting with them in a way that has monumental potential for their growth. Again, the purpose of the attraction series is to get people to come to your church during the times of the year when they are naturally most likely to do so. Cooperate with the calendar and get them on deck. Then relate to them in a way that keeps them coming back for more so you can move them toward a relationship with Jesus and a radically transformed life. (For a list of attraction series suggestions, visit www.ChurchLeaderInsights.com/Engage.)

Growth series. Growth series are your power hitters. They are commitment series that are focused on helping people become more like Jesus. Growth series lead to RTLs by spurring both new attenders and regular attenders/members to take the next steps in their spiritual growth. They are already on base, so now you begin to dig deeper and bring them home. Growth series should be positioned during those times of year when your attendance is naturally the highest and steadiest over a period of months.

Here's how a growth series functions, practically speaking. Imagine that you are planning to do a big attraction series in February. Once the series is over, you have March and part of April available before you do another attraction series kickoff on Easter Sunday. You should use that period of time to focus on a topic designed to grow your people—to help believers become more like Jesus and invite unbelievers to step into a relationship with him. Consider doing a series on the Beatitudes, prayer, key figures in the New Testament, or something similar that will resonate with your listeners. (For a list of growth series suggestions, visit www.ChurchLeaderInsights.com/Engage.)

Balance series. Balance series accomplish just what the name implies. They bring balance to your overall calendar. In a baseball lineup, these are the guys who even out the playing field.

74

In your lineup, balance series do something similar. These are the series that deal with important, non-attraction, nongrowth topics you want to address—the various issues that come up in your church that you aren't able to work into other times of the year. Balance series are meant to help your regular attenders and members mature. At the same time, they give unbelievers in your midst an inside look at what it means to be a Christian.

Recently, at The Journey, we did an extremely well-received balance series called "Accelerate." Over the course of five weeks, we discussed topics such as how to study your Bible, how to pray, the power of generosity, how to create solitude in a busy life, and how God uses friendships for spiritual growth. These are topics we wanted to talk about with our people that wouldn't naturally attract unbelievers and wouldn't necessarily qualify as a power-hitting growth series. They are simply issues our members and regular attenders are interested in and necessary to their continuing journey toward becoming fully developing followers of Jesus.

Position your balance series at those times of the year when your attendance fluctuates the most. Since you may not have all your attenders around every week, you have some freedom to group loosely connected topics into a series. While every message in the series should be crafted around the same theme, not every message has to build on the one before it. For example, in the past, we have had people submit questions they would like to have answered and built a series around those. Each week is different, but they all fall under the same "Your Questions Answered" theme. (For a list of balance series suggestions, visit www.ChurchLeaderInsights.com/Engage.)

Below you will find an example of how to plan your message series throughout the year.

Month	Series Type	Key Words
January	growth or balance	core values
February	attraction	felt needs
March	growth	maturity
April/Easter	attraction	life application
May	growth or balance	depth
June/July	attraction or growth	stand alone
August	balance	issue related
September/October	attraction or growth	spiritual adventure
November/December	balance or growth	inspiration

At first, I thought, "How could God really speak to me if I had everything already planned out?" What I didn't understand was that God speaks when I am better prepared. This has helped the entire flow and direction of the church and taken a lot of last-minute preparation and worry out of the planning.

Marty Macdonald, Pastor
City Church, Batavia, New York

Step 3: Prayerfully Set Your Calendar

The third step of planning your preaching calendar is one that should actually begin before step 1 and carry through step 2 and beyond. Prayer is an essential component throughout this process. Planning is a spiritual enterprise. God is the only one who knows how your calendar should shape up over the course of the next year. As you begin to piece it together, make sure you seek his wisdom and guidance at every turn. Ask him to bring the topics he wants you to address to your mind. Listen as he guides you to place them at certain points in the year. God wants to use his Holy Spirit to guide you into his perfect plan for your church. Take the time to connect with him in prayer. (To learn more about how to prepare your preaching,

download my free ebook *Before You Step on Stage* at www
.ChurchLeaderInsights.com/Engage.)

Never forget that you have the incredible privilege of cooperating with the one who charted the universe. Give him
room and permission to map your preaching for his purposes,
as you fulfill your obligation to be an excellent representation
of his nature. As Charles Spurgeon illustrates so powerfully
with the following words, you and I are called to prayerfully
plan and execute our preaching and then leave the rest up to
the Master:

> The power that is in the gospel does not lie in the eloquence of
> the preacher; otherwise men would be the converters of souls.
> Nor does it lie in the preacher's learning; otherwise it would
> consist in the wisdom of men. We might preach until our tongues
> rotted, till we would exhaust our lungs and die, but never a soul
> would be converted unless the Holy Spirit be with the Word of
> God to give it the power to convert the soul.

Preaching Calendar Example

January

3—Beyond GPS: Knowing and Doing the Will of God: Kickoff
Learning to Hear

10—Learning to Trust
Spring Growth Group sign-ups begin

17—Staying on Course (Three Big Things That Get Us Off Track: Money, Rela-
tionships, Career)
Martin Luther King Jr. weekend
Nelson out

24—U-Turns Allowed/No Dead Ends
Spring Growth Group leader training

31—Pure Sex: Kickoff
100 Percent Pure
Journey members' meeting

February

7—Thought Filters
Super Bowl Sunday
Newcomers' reception
Spring Growth Groups begin this week

14—Dating Filters
Valentine's Day and Presidents' Day Weekend
Promote fast for Lent
Nelson out
17—Ash Wednesday (Kickoff of Lent)

21—Marriage Filters
Membership class

28—Pure Forgiveness
Baptism

March

7—Fruits of the Spirit (Part 1): Kickoff
Love
Worship Arts Team reception

14—Joy
Daylight Savings Time begins (clocks forward an hour)

21—Peace
Worship Arts Team auditions

28—Patience
Membership class
March 29–April 3—Spring Growth Group Servant Evangelism Week

April

4—Easter Sunday—Unshakable Faith: Kickoff
Building a Rock-Solid Faith in a Shaky World

11—Facing Failure with Faith
Newcomers' reception

18—Facing Death with Faith
Worship Arts Team new season orientation
April 22—Earth Day

25—Facing Doubt with Faith
> Nelson out
> Membership class

May

2—Facing Illness with Faith
> Baptism

9—Family Day
> Mother's Day
> Family portraits

16—Living with Unshakable Faith (Because Jesus Is Alive, You Can . . .)
> Summer Growth Groups sign-ups begin

Nelson sabbatical **May 16–August 22**

23—TBD

30—TBD
> Combined service
> Memorial Day weekend

June

6—God on Film: Kickoff
> Summer Growth Group leader training

13—Film TBD
> Newcomers' reception
> Summer Growth Groups begin this week

20—Film TBD
> Father's Day
> Membership class

27—Film TBD

July

4—Film TBD
> Combined services
> Fourth of July weekend

11—Film TBD

July 12–17—Summer Growth Group Servant Evangelism Week

18——Film TBD
> Membership class

25—Film TBD
July 31—Beach baptism

1—**Fruits of the Spirit (Part 2): Kickoff**
   Kindness

8—**Goodness**

15—**Faithfulness**
   Worship Arts Team reception

22—**Gentleness**
   Membership class

29—**Self-Control**
   Worship Arts Team auditions

5—**Smart Money: Kickoff**
   Intelligent Spending
   Labor Day weekend
   Fall Growth Groups sign-ups begin

12—**Intelligent Debt Reduction**
   Worship Arts Team new season orientation
September 14—Membership class

19—**Intelligent Generosity**
   Fall Growth Group leader training

26—**Intelligent Crisis Management**
   Baptism

3—**Forty Days with Jesus: Kickoff**
   The High Cost of Following Jesus (Matt. 5:3)
   Newcomers' reception

10—**Jesus on Problems (Matt. 5:4)**
   Nelson out
   Columbus Day weekend

17—**Jesus on Success (Matt. 5:5)**
   Membership class

24—**Jesus on Justice (Matt. 5:6)**
October 25–30—Fall Growth Group Servant Evangelism Week

31—Jesus on Compassion (Matt. 5:7)
   Journey Kidz Fall Festival

November

7—Jesus on Purity (Matt. 5:8)
   Daylight Savings Time ends (clocks back an hour)
   Journey members' reception
November 11—Veterans Day

14—Jesus on Peace (Matt. 5:9)
   Membership class
November 16—Special worship night and baptism

21—Living with Jesus (Matt. 5:10)
November 25—Thanksgiving

28—Four Gifts God Has for You This Christmas: Kickoff
   God's Gift of Purpose for You
   Nelson out

December

5—God's Gift of Strength for You
   Newcomers' reception
   Nelson out

12—God's Gift of Joy for You
   Membership class

19—God's Gift of Hope for You
   Leaders' Christmas party
December 25—Christmas Day

26—No services

5

preaching
for life transformation

Tips and Temptations

The pulpit calls those anointed to it like the sea calls its sailor;
and like the sea, it batters and bruises, and does not rest. . . . To
preach, to really preach, is to die naked a little at a time, and to
know each time you do it that you must do it again.

Bruce Thielemann

We plan the way we want to live,
but only God makes us able to live it.

Proverbs 16:9 Message

As Tim signs the receipt and takes one last swig of coffee,
he senses David still has some questions. "How's the
rest of your day shaping up?" Tim asks.

Snapping out of his thoughts, David says, "Oh, I have a meeting with Sarah, our worship pastor, and a few other things I need
to tackle after that, but . . . but now, I may shift my schedule and

spend some time thinking through this whole idea of planning my preaching in advance."

"That's a good idea, David. You could start by looking at your calendar and some of your past attendance records and identifying the trends. When you actually get down to the planning, though, it's not something to be taken lightly. Planning a preaching calendar is a prayerful endeavor."

"You know, it makes sense. I believe God is all-knowing. He already knows what's going to happen every day between now and eternity. So why wouldn't I think that he could speak to me in advance about a message or a series? I can't believe I thought that waiting until the last minute was giving him more room to work. I've actually been squelching his freedom by not inviting him to speak to me earlier! Tim, this is good stuff. I feel like I am seeing things in a whole new way."

Tim can't help but smile at David's realization. "That's exactly right. When guys like you and me learn to cooperate with the Holy Spirit by planning in advance, we get to be part of something incredible—we get to see lives being radically transformed every single week."

David settles back into the booth. "So I pretty much understand how to start sketching out my calendar. What else do I need to know?"

"Do you have a few more minutes?" Tim asks.

David glances at his watch. "Sure. My meeting isn't for another hour."

"Okay, well, here are a few tips I've discovered through years of planning my calendar in advance." Tim pulls out his planner, rips out a sheet of paper, and begins jotting down some notes.

Tips

Tip 1: Schedule a yearly time away to work on your preaching calendar. I know your schedule is packed, but if you can get in the habit of blocking out a few days every year to get away from the office, seek God, and sketch out your preaching calendar for the next year, you will have a much better planning experience. At The Journey, we try to have a planning retreat once a year with all the teaching and worship pastors for this very purpose. We spend the time praying, brainstorming, and piecing together our calendar for the next twelve months. While this kind of retreat is highly beneficial to your planning, don't let it become a barrier. If you can't get away, simply plan a series of meetings at your office to pray over your calendar and talk through message ideas.

Tip 2: Pray and fast before and/or during your planning time. You need to be absolutely sure you are in a position to hear from God during your planning time. If you are doing a retreat, ask everyone going with you to fast and pray before leaving as they seek God's direction on what the next year holds.

Tip 3: Consult a school calendar and a regular calendar that notes all key holidays. As we've established, the school calendar in your area will have a huge impact on your year. Make sure you bring a copy of this calendar to your planning sessions. You will also need to consult a calendar that notes key holidays and important cultural dates. When you walk into a planning session, you have to know things like when Memorial Day weekend falls and when Columbus Day is, especially if the kids in your area will have a three-day weekend. This will keep you from making the mistake of planning a big service when many families may not be in church.

To that end, you need to know when Super Bowl Sunday is. I've known many pastors who make the "spiritual" choice to ignore realities like Super Bowl Sunday. Here's something I can guarantee: unbelievers won't come to your church for the first time on Super Bowl Sunday. If you kick off your February attraction series that day, you will be penalizing yourself—and all the people you would have liked to reach. You will be throwing a stumbling block in their way. Why would you want to do that when you can just as easily kick off the next week? Don't fight the calendar. Remove your blinders and work with it.

Tip 4: Examine your attendance trends from the previous two years. Examine the data and determine when your highest days, lowest days, and most sporadic days are so you can plan your preaching calendar accordingly. When we first started The Journey, many well-intentioned people told me that Labor Day would be a low Sunday. So, working from assumption rather than fact, I scheduled a guest speaker for Labor Day weekend. (Low attendance Sundays are a good time to bring in a guest speaker and give yourself a Sunday off.) Then one day I was examining our attendance trends, and I realized that Labor Day Sunday is actually a pretty big day in our community. Now I've restructured our service schedule to reflect that. The numbers are your friends. Pay attention to them.

Tip 5: Plan as a team. Never forget the importance of synergy. God will use your entire leadership team in the planning process, if you will let him. Revisit the W of our WORSHIP philosophy in chapter 2 for a refresher on the importance of this tip.

Tip 6: Brainstorm key series topics or issues. Pull out a whiteboard or a piece of paper, gather your team, and brainstorm topics you might be interested in addressing in the upcoming year. Nothing is off-limits in a brainstorming session. Even the craziest ideas can lead you down the right path. I always like to come to our planning time with some issues in mind that I feel we should add to the mix. For example, one year I couldn't shake the feeling that we needed to address the issue of divorce. I brought that into the brainstorming session, and we worked a message on divorce into a series called "Relationship Rescue."

Tip 7: Outline the start dates and end dates for each message series. Be sure to include guest speakers, holidays, and standalone messages as you lay out your series dates. To get started, focus initially on the February attraction series and on the attraction series you'll kick off one month after school begins in your area. These two important series will help anchor and guide all your other planning.

Tip 8: Keep all unused ideas for the future. If you come across a good idea in a planning meeting but don't think you'll be able to work it into the coming year's calendar, file it away for the future. God may have given you that seed for another time. Revisit your ideas file every time you begin planning for a new year.

Tip 9: Don't worry if there are gaps. You may have series dates laid out for a growth series or a balance series but have no idea what the topic is going to be. Or maybe you know the overall topic, but you aren't sure about the individual messages. Just keep moving. Keep planning. Get as many pieces of the puzzle in place as you can and then work to fill in the gaps later.

Tip 10: Don't forget to schedule the times you will be away. You can't be fresh fifty-two weeks of the year. Make sure you plan vacation time into your preaching calendar. This may be a difficult step. You may struggle with the idea of not preaching every Sunday. At the very least, decide to preach only fifty of the fifty-two weeks in the coming year. The next year, you could move that number down to forty-five and begin raising up some new teachers. (For more information on balancing your time, check out the "Developing a One-Year Personal Growth Plan" audio resource at www.ChurchLeaderInsights.com/Engage.)

Tip 11: Set aside the draft calendar for a couple of weeks and then revisit it. Piece your preaching calendar together during your planning time, then set it aside for a couple of weeks. Get some distance from the details as you continue to cover them in prayer. Then reexamine your calendar and make sure you still feel good about your plan.

Tip 12: Revisit the calendar as often as needed to stay two to three months ahead. Make sure you are always working two to three months ahead. We'll talk more about how to set up your service planning timelines in the next chapter.

Tip 13: Allow God to interrupt your calendar. Not too long ago we were planning our preaching calendar for an upcoming year, and we had a period of time in May we weren't sure how to handle. We had a few ideas but nothing solid. In the midst of praying over the calendar, we felt God was leading us to spend three weeks on Cain and Abel. This didn't make sense in our minds. There are only a few verses on Cain and Abel—hardly enough to build a three-part series around. But we felt God was directing us, so we moved ahead. We built an entire series around Cain and Abel's story, and it was incredibly well received. Let God interrupt your calendar. He knows what's best.

All these tips will help you plan your preaching for maximum impact. They will help to ensure that you are planning in a way that both engages God's power and will engage the people you will be speaking to. But I would be remiss to give you good tips and not make you aware of the accompanying temptations that lurk about in the world of planning. The following three temptations lead to pitfalls. Beware.

Temptations

Temptation 1: Wait until the last minute. Planning your preaching calendar takes a lot of discipline at the beginning, but in the end it leads to life-transforming services—not to mention, it saves you time, trouble, and stress every week. Waiting until the last minute to plan will hurt both you and your people.

Temptation 2: Plan your preaching alone. We've already covered this in some detail. Don't fall into the temptation of planning by yourself. Let God use the creative souls he has placed around you. When you plan alone, you get only your ideas. The problem is, your ideas may not be the best ideas. Don't get me wrong, mine aren't either! That's why you and I need a team of people around us to interact with our ideas and to bring fresh perspectives to the table. By accepting input from the people God has placed around you, you will create a sharper, more in-tune preaching calendar.

Temptation 3: Change what has already been planned. Every pastor is sometimes tempted to change a message at the last minute. But if you have planned prayerfully and properly—trusting that God knows the exact message that needs to be preached at the exact moment it needs to be preached—you should never change your message based on last-minute feelings or circumstances. Every time I have given in to this temptation, I've regretted it. Plan your preaching and then trust God as each week approaches. (To learn more about creating your preaching calendar, download the free "Planning a One-Year Preaching Calendar" audio resource at www.ChurchLeaderInsights.com/Engage.)

David folds the piece of paper and sticks it in his bag as the two men slide out of the booth and head to the door.

"Ah, dry skies," Tim comments and tucks his umbrella under his arm.

"Listen, Tim," David says. "Is it okay if I give you a call as I keep thinking through all of this?"

"Of course," says Tim. "Let me know if you have any other questions. Just remember this, David. You have some kind of planning system now. You already plan your preaching a certain way. Changing your method to cooperate with God for more RTLs won't be that much more work. It just takes a shift in perspective and some front-end diligence."

"Yeah, I get that. And, honestly, it's no picnic planning the way I'm planning now, and not even worth it if people are forgetting what I've said right away."

"Right," Tim agrees. "And you know what else? Your worship leader will thank you for this. Speaking of which, you better get to your meeting!"

"Thanks, Tim! See you next month. Same time, same place," David says as he heads to his car.

"Yep, see you then!" Tim watches David jump in his car and head out of the parking lot. As he settles into his own driver's seat, he thanks God for letting him be a part of such incredible, eternity-altering work.

Coming from a traditional church background, I always felt that if I would do a little studying on a specific topic, the Holy Spirit would lead my preaching to hit the right points and impact the lives of our members. I had little regard for seasons, times of year, or what our members were naturally experiencing. I just worked very hard trying to connect during my preaching. Since implementing a preaching calendar that takes into account the seasons, times of year, and natural state of our members, we have seen results worth celebrating. I have discovered that the Holy Spirit works with me better during my advance planning than when I was less prepared. He reveals biblical application principles to me that directly address the needs and concerns of our members.

Gadville McDonald, Pastor
Life Empowerment Church, Nassau, Bahamas

planning
and conducting
worship services

6

below the waterline

Building Your Worship Planning System

The dignity of movement of an iceberg is due to only one ninth
of it being above water.

Ernest Hemingway

Work hard so you can present yourself to God and receive his approval. Be a good worker, one who does not need to be ashamed
and who correctly explains the word of truth.

2 Timothy 2:15

Icebergs are glorious pieces of nature that have mystified
observers for centuries. With tips ranging from the size of
a grand piano to the size of a ten-story building, these floating
chunks of ice take on various fascinating shapes and configura-

tions. Yet as majestic as icebergs seem to us, what you and I are able to see is only a small sliver of the whole. Ninety percent of an iceberg's mass lies beneath the water. This hidden base determines every detail of the tip's size and composition. The piece of ice that breaks the waterline is merely a manifestation of what's happening in the deep and wouldn't even exist without the power of the structure below.

Your Sunday service is like the tip of a massive iceberg. The planning and preparation going on beneath the surface will determine the shape, strength, and overall impact of the hour or so you have with your people. Think about it: your service is the only visible manifestation of your hard work, prayer, and planning; it's often the only thing your people see. They don't see what goes on in your office during the week. They don't see the sweat that goes into creating the atmosphere they walk into on Sunday mornings. All they see is the service your planning system produces—the small piece of the whole that pushes above the waterline.

If the goal of your preaching is to connect God's truth to real life in a way that leads to transformation, then it's safe to infer that your overarching goal will be to create a life-transforming worship service each Sunday. You don't preach in a void. Being able to connect truth to people's lives in a radically transforming way is intertwined with and largely dependent on your ability to design effective worship services. You have to have a system at work in the deep that is capable of creating engaging, powerful, awe-inspiring services each Sunday. Again, the tip your people will experience is the direct result of the volume and quality of your base. That volume and quality are comprised of your worship planning system.

A Different Way to Live

In the life of the average pastor or worship pastor, a funny thing happens every Monday morning. He wakes up, and it occurs to him that he has a service on Sunday. He's not sure why it didn't occur to him earlier; he's not sure why he didn't think of it the week before. But for whatever reason, on Monday morning, it hits him. So he works hard all week to get ready for the service. He busts his tail to write a message or put together a worship set, to get props and illustrations ready or pull together the worship order, to recruit volunteers or get the music charts written, to create the PowerPoint slides or fill in the empty spots on the roster. Sometime late Friday night, he catches his breath and thinks to himself, "Okay, it's done. I think we have it all together."

On Saturday, this average pastor or worship pastor wakes up nervous. Saturday is likely his Sabbath, and he should be resting, but instead he's worried: Did I research that point well enough? Is the vocalist going to learn those words? Is that story going to fly? Is the guitar player going to have time to learn the solo? Are the transitions going to be smooth? On Sunday morning, he wakes up closer to God than he has been all week. All morning he prays, "Dear Lord, please let this service come together without the wheels falling off. Please help the service to be good today. Please meet us there. Please work it all out." He gets to church and conducts the service. Some mistakes are made, some things get missed, but overall the service goes well, and he considers it a success. He heads home on Sunday afternoon, has some lunch, wipes the sweat off his brow, and says to himself, "Whew! We made it through." Then on Monday morning, he wakes up, and it occurs to him that he has a service on Sunday.

There is another way to live. Can you imagine going into Sunday knowing you are completely prepared, confident you aren't leaving anything to chance? Consider how it would feel to approach each week knowing that you've heard from the Holy Spirit, that you have cooperated with God to do your part in creating a great service for his people, that he is going to meet you there and work through the details of the environment he has prompted you to design. Does that level of preparedness sound out of reach? It's not. With an effective worship planning system in place, you can break the cycle of weekly pressure and walk into every Sunday with peace and confidence. (To learn more about breaking the week-to-week mentality, download the free *Overcoming the Seven Challenges of a Worship Pastor* ebook at www.ChurchLeaderInsights.com/Engage.)

Setting Timelines

The first step in creating a worship planning system that produces life-transforming services is to determine your philosophy of worship. The second step is to plan your preaching calendar. Once you have prayerfully worked through those two steps, there's only one thing left to do: get ready for next Sunday's service . . . and the service the Sunday after that and the Sunday after that. The nitty-gritty details of how you plan and implement your services each week will form the bulk of your worship planning system.

Take a few minutes to think through how your ideal planning process would look. To do so, consider how you would like to answer these three questions, in a perfect world:

1. How far in advance do you plan each series?
   (When do you have titles, topics, graphics, and key Scripture passages ready?)

2. How far in advance do you plan each message?
(When do you have titles, Scripture passages, creative elements, and specific outlines ready?)
3. How far in advance do you finalize each Sunday?
(When do you have the worship order and creative elements ready?)

To help you work through these questions, let me give you an idea of the worship planning timelines we use at The Journey. Yes, that's plural. We have established two timelines that work together to define the logistics of our worship planning system.

1. Timeline for message series planning. This is the timeline that flows out of the preaching calendar, helping us to maximize the effectiveness of a series by planning in advance.
2. Timeline for specific Sunday planning. This is the timeline for each individual Sunday. It keeps us on track with all the last-minute details for a specific service.

I'll be the first to tell you that we don't always hit the time frames we've set for ourselves. But experience has taught us that if we don't define the ideal, we will never get close to it with the real—and neither will you. In an ideal world, if everything happened according to schedule, our series and service planning would unfold as follows.

Message Series Timeline

Four to ten months out: *finalize the series ideas and/or series titles.* Imagine that at our preaching calendar planning retreat, we decided to do a growth series on theology during a specific four-week period. Four to ten months before that series is scheduled to begin, we would nail down the overall series concept and title. For example, let's say we decide to do a series focusing specifically on the theology of discipleship, centered on the "I am" passages in John 14. We decide that the series title is going to be "iGod."

Six weeks to one month out: *finalize the individual message titles and the series theme.* Since our "iGod" series is based on John 14, we decide on four message titles that play on the "I am" concept:

1. I God am all present.
2. I God am all powerful.
3. I God am all knowing.
4. I God am all loving.

Begin collecting creative materials based on the titles and theme you've established. Think about songs, movie clips, testimonies, or drama elements that could support the message. (See chap. 7 for a detailed discussion on using creative elements in your service.)

Begin the design process. The first goal of the design process is to create a series postcard. Once the series postcard is created and approved, we lift elements from it to construct the look and feel of the entire message series. (To learn more about the timeline for designing a series postcard, download the free "Design Time Line" at www.ChurchLeaderInsights.com/Engage.) The design drives our staging and influences the look of our programs, PowerPoint graphics, memory verse cards, and even a portion of our website for the duration of the series. Don't neglect the power of integration. (For information on using series postcards and theme integration to raise the evangelistic temperature in your church, see my previous book *Ignite: How to Spark Immediate Growth in Your Church* [Baker, 2009].)

One month out: hold a creative planning meeting. At some point, you may have an actual creative team, but if you aren't there yet, just tap into the creative talents of a few key members and regular attenders. Invite them to an evening meeting at the church, review the upcoming series theme, and then give them room to be creative. See what they come up with to support the series concept. The best creative planning meetings happen when those in attendance know the series topic in advance and arrive with some ideas already formulated. When everyone comes prepared, the synergy in the room pushes the best ideas to the top and then makes them even better. Plan a time after the meeting to sit down with your worship pastor and sort through the ideas. Use what works; discard what doesn't. For reference, make sure you have a list of important dates—baptisms, membership classes, holidays, and the like—available at this meeting. (To see notes from an actual creative planning meeting, go to www.ChurchLeaderInsights.com/Engage.)

Ten days out: finalize any series specific staging and test potential props. Our goal is to have all the staging elements for an upcoming series finalized by midnight on Thursday, the week before kickoff. That way we can test everything before the Sunday kickoff.

> *Before we started using the worship planning system, we used to come up with all the creative ideas used in our weekend services*

on our own. Needless to say, our ideas were limited. Once we learned about having a creative planning meeting, we decided to give it a try. Our worship pastor held a one-hour meeting with a handful of people who had suggested creative ideas in the past. The results were amazing! More creative ideas came out of that single one-hour meeting than we could have come up with in ten! Since then, we have held a creative planning meeting before each upcoming series. We have started calling them "Blue Sky Creative Sessions." ("Blue Sky" is a Disney phrase basically meaning "The sky is the limit.") We are no longer scrambling to put together half-baked creative ideas for our services! What a difference!

Gabe Kolstad, Lead Pastor
Westside Community Church, Beaverton, Oregon

The message series time line parallels our specific Sunday time line. Each individual Sunday comes together (ideally) via the following schedule.

Specific Sunday Timeline

Three weeks out: *finalize message research and study (teaching pastor).* Imagine the specific Sunday we are planning for is week two of the "iGod" series, "I God am all powerful." By three weeks out, the teaching pastor/teaching team will know all the key Scripture passages and quotations we are planning to use to illustrate the fact that God is all powerful. We will know what major theologians have said about the omnipotence of God. We will have studied commentaries. In short, we will have gathered and dissected all the research that's pertinent to the "I God am all powerful" assertion.

103

Two weeks out: plan specific music and creative elements that will be used in the service (worship pastor). What songs will support "I God am all powerful"? What movie clips illustrate the message point? Are there any testimonies that might work well? (Again, see chap. 7.) (To learn more about planning music as a team, check out the "Leading with Authority in Rehearsal" resource at www.ChurchLeaderInsights.com/Engage.)

Two weeks to ten days out: hold a worship planning meeting. Turn in the first draft of the message notes during the meeting (teaching pastor). The worship planning meeting is simply a time when the teaching pastor, worship pastor, and other key people talk through the direction for Sunday. It is an opportunity to confirm that everyone is on the same page and has everything he or she needs to continue planning effectively. Short worship planning meetings can go a long way. Note that you can also use part of the time to look toward the future. In our worship planning meetings, we spend about 85 percent of the time talking about the specific Sunday in question and the other 15 percent talking about services further down the road.

Finalize and turn in a first draft of the worship order (worship pastor). Remember that the message drives the day. By default, this means that the message drives the worship order. Certain types of worship orders work more effectively with certain messages. Every Sunday doesn't have to look like the Sunday before. In fact, your services will be more effective if they don't follow the same pattern week to week. (See www .ChurchLeaderInsights.com/Engage for more details and examples of worship orders.) We use three types of worship orders at The Journey.

1. Simple. In a simple worship order, the worship leader controls the first half of the service, while the teaching pastor controls the second half of the service. At The Journey, about 70 percent of our services are simple.

Simple Worship Order

Preview video
Worship team—worship songs
    3–4 songs
Host—welcome/greet/connection card
Worship team—worship songs
    1–2 songs
Video roll-in
Teaching pastor—message/prayer/next steps
Possible video clip or testimony used during message
Host—Important information/offering

2. Split. In a split worship order, control of the service begins with the worship leader, shifts to the teaching pastor, goes back to the worship leader, and finally rests with the teaching pastor. For example, the worship leader leads the congregation in two or three songs; the teaching pastor teaches the first part of his message; the worship pastor comes back with another two songs in the middle of the message; the teaching pastor wraps up with the second part of the message. At The Journey, we use a split worship order about 25 percent of the time.

Split Worship Order

Preview video
Worship team—worship songs

2–3 songs
Host—welcome/greet/connection card
Video/drama/arts
Worship team—worship songs
    2 songs
Video roll-in
Teaching pastor—message (part 1)
Worship team—worship songs
    2 songs
Teaching pastor—message (part 2)/prayer/next steps
Host—Important information/offering

3. Salsa. In a salsa worship order, control rotates continu-
ously between the worship leader and the teaching pastor
throughout the service. We use a salsa worship order in
about 5 percent of our services.

Salsa Worship Order

Preview video
Worship team—worship songs
    2–3 songs
Host—welcome/greet/connection card
Video roll-in
Teaching pastor—message (point 1)
Worship team—worship songs
    2 songs
Teaching pastor—message (point 2)
Music/video/drama/arts
Teaching pastor—message (point 3)
Worship team—worship song
Host—Important information/offering

Ten days out: finalize the music and make it available to the worship team (worship pastor).

Five days out: turn in the final draft of the message notes (teaching pastor). Turn in the final draft of the worship order and creative elements (worship pastor). If we haven't already begun praying specifically and intentionally for this service, we begin now. We actually use the finalized worship order as our prayer guide for the next several days. We pray for specific parts of the service and the transitions in between. We pray for the people who will be sitting in the crowd. We pray for the offering. We pray for the specific responsibilities that our volunteers and staff will have. Every service should be bathed in prayer.

Three days out: hold a production meeting to go over everything for Sunday. Invite the key people who are going to be involved in the Sunday service and use the time to talk specifically through production cues and transitions.

Finalize the message manuscript and conduct a message run-through (teaching pastor). Doing a run-through of your message before Sunday is critical. You need to practice flying a plane in a simulator before you take it to twenty-five thousand feet. (See chap. 8 for a detailed discussion of the message run-through.)

Make sure everything for Sunday is finalized (teaching pastor and worship pastor). We don't always hit the goal of having everything ready by midnight on Thursday, but we are successful about 60 percent of the time. Simply aiming for it makes all the difference. Whether or not you choose to set a Thursday midnight rule for yourself isn't what's important. The important thing is that you implement a specific deadline—one with plenty of margin—for when you will have everything ready for your service.

For your timelines to run smoothly—and for the entire worship planning system to function effectively—it's important to adhere to four requirements:

1. High accountability among staff and volunteers. Don't be afraid to hold both your staff and your volunteers to a high level of accountability. You have to set the bar and stick to it. If the drama team hasn't rehearsed their piece by Thursday night at midnight, they don't get to do the drama on Sunday. If someone who is supposed to give a testimony doesn't have his manuscript in by midnight on Thursday, he doesn't get to do the testimony on Sunday. The first couple of times you enforce strict accountability, it is going to hurt. But then everyone will get the point and move toward personal accountability and excellence.

2. A culture of punctuality. Punctuality comes down to discipline. Discipline yourself to get the teaching notes in on time; make sure the worship order is in on time. For the sake of keeping your timelines on schedule, do your best to meet all your deadlines.

3. A commitment to excellence. If everyone is devoted to honoring God on Sunday—to glorifying his name as best as possible—cultivating a commitment to excellence won't be a problem.

4. Constant conversation between the teaching pastor and the worship pastor. If there are issues between the teaching pastor and the worship pastor, they will show up on the stage. Keep this relationship strong. (See chap. 9 for a detailed discussion of the pastor/worship pastor relationship.)

Constantly Cultivate Clarity

Precise timelines—especially when strengthened by the four requirements of an effective worship planning system—allow you to constantly cultivate clarity. They lead to clear communication, careful planning, and captivating services. Your timelines don't have to look exactly like the ones we use at The Journey, but you do need to put timelines in place—one for your message series planning and one for your specific Sunday service planning—if you have any desire to create powerful, engaging worship services. Take a look at how being clear and establishing these timelines created a big win on a Sunday at The Journey.

A few years ago, as I mentioned, we did a series called "Relationship Rescue." The series focused on repairing the broken relationships in our lives. It dealt with intimate topics such as family, dating, and divorce. For the kickoff Sunday of the series, Jason wanted to do a song from the Broadway musical *Rent* called "Seasons of Love." The song is incredibly powerful, focusing on the love—and the time—that makes up a life. There was only one problem: *Rent* was playing on Broadway just six blocks north of where we were meeting at the time. If we were going to tackle this difficult song for the service, it could not be subpar. It had to be every bit as good as what was on the Broadway stage a few blocks away.

Jason brought the idea for "Seasons of Love" to our creative planning meeting a month before the series began. We decided to give it a shot, and the preparations began. Jason's team had to track down some of the instruments, rearrange a few schedules to get just the right singers for the day, hold two extra vocal team rehearsals, and hold a longer than usual band rehearsal to get the song ready. All in all, it took three weeks to pull the piece together. Was it worth it? Well, when they performed the song on Sunday, they did so to a standing ovation at every service. Our new series kicked off with a bang. What would have happened if we had not held that creative planning meeting? What if the idea to do "Seasons of Love" hadn't come to us until the Monday morning before the Sunday service? I'll tell you what would have happened: a major missed opportunity. We wouldn't have been able to pull it together; we would have missed out on an extremely powerful experience in our worship service.

Clarity is key. If your services aren't clear to you in advance, they won't be clear to your attenders on the day in question, which means they won't lead to radically transformed lives. But as you lift the fog of confusion by pursuing clarity—and as you shape and strengthen your system by choosing to be diligent in your worship planning—you will reveal the tip of a glorious, awe-inspiring, life-transforming iceberg.

Worship has always been an important part of our church community, but so have all the board meetings, committee meetings, visitations, and the rest of my responsibilities as pastor. When it came to "planning" for worship, it just didn't happen. If we did plan, it was on a very small scale and it showed! The worship planning system has now become one of the most instrumental components of our new vision. Instead of going week by week, we are now planning our teaching series, music, and staging months in advance. This has helped us to have a more meaningful worship experience for our members but more importantly for our first- and second-time guests. The system also makes things a lot less stressful for me.

Neil Partington, Pastor
First Congregational Church, Lake Mills, Wisconsin

7

creative transformation

Aligning Creative Elements for Excellence

The whole is greater than the sum of its parts.

Aristotle

So then neither the one who plants nor the one who waters is anything, but God who causes the growth.

1 Corinthians 3:7 NASB

Tim pulls into the parking lot of his church, FCC, and notices Scott, the worship pastor, standing off to the side of the church building with four or five other people. Tim parks and heads over to the group. As he gets closer he sees that one of the guys is holding a video camera. Then he notices a young couple pinning small microphones to their shirts. Tim remembers that Scott and his team are shooting a video testimony today for the service two weeks from now. Scott sees Tim approaching and walks over.

"Hey, Tim!" says Scott. "How's it going?"

"Good, Scott! You guys are setting up to shoot a testimony, huh?"

"Yep. You are going to love this couple's story—really powerful stuff. This is for Sunday after next—the 'I God am all loving' service," answers Scott.

"That's right. I remember talking about this testimony in the creative planning meeting last month. You know I always love a strong video testimony! Is there anything you need from me?"

"No, I think we've got it covered." Scott glances over his shoulder and notices the couple and the camera guy getting in position to shoot. "I better get back over there, but I may drop by your office later to connect on a couple of things. Will you be around?"

"Yep, I'll be here. I'm going to spend the afternoon finalizing Sunday's manuscript. Stop by anytime," says Tim. Turning to walk away, Tim gives a wave to the group working on the video. "Can't wait to see it, guys!" he calls out, and then heads toward the building.

As we saw in the last chapter, part of your worship planning process involves pulling together creative elements that can strengthen your service—expressive components that illustrate and underscore the message you want your people to take away with them. Seven specific elements have the potential to make your service powerful). The first two are no-brainers: music and the message.

Music and the message are the yin and yang of every worship service. You have to have these two elements in place to have a service at all. My team and I like to debate which one is the most important, but the reality is that they work together for God's glory, each strengthening and informing the other. At the bare minimum, make sure your worship services contain both well-planned music and biblical teaching. The other five creative elements we'll discuss can be used at your will. While the synergy between these elements can create a strong worship service, some of them have much greater resonance than others. So let's look at each potential creative element, in order of potential impact.

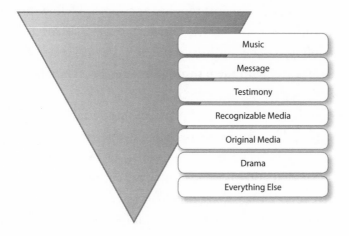

Creative Elements

Music

The psalmist tells us that God inhabits the praises of his people (Ps. 22:3 KJV). Accordingly, I believe that music opens people's hearts to hear from him. As God indwells the praises of his people, they are drawn into his presence. Their defenses are lowered. Their hearts attune to his. The importance of well-planned, intentional music in a worship service can't be underestimated; it is essential to helping your people connect with God and hear what he wants to say to them.

In addition to singing songs during the service, you can incorporate music into your service in another way. At The Journey, we have discovered that there is power in playing a secular song as people leave the service—something that is applicable to the message they've just heard. I have a theory that if you take a secular song and reframe it around a theological idea, that idea will lodge in people's minds on an even deeper level. For example, if I have just taught a message on fellowship and community, we may play the Pointer Sisters' "We Are Family" as people leave the auditorium. The tune will catch in their minds and stay with them throughout the day, reminding them of what they learned in church.

Recently, I taught on the Ephesians passage about husbands respecting their wives. As people left the service, we played Aretha Franklin's "Respect." Many men have told me that when they hear that song now, it reminds them of the biblical imperative to love their wives as Christ loved the church. As Paul knew and demonstrated in his day, taking the things of culture and reframing them around biblical principles goes a long way. Don't fight the culture your people live in; use it.

Message

Consistent, biblical teaching is critical to the development of Christ followers. As Paul tells his young disciple Timothy, "Give attention to the public reading of Scripture, to exhortation and

116

teaching" (1 Tim. 4:13 NASB). You can't cooperate with God to help the people he has entrusted to you become more like his Son without a strong, grounded plan for your preaching. Since the message is so important, I strongly encourage you to do a message run-through every week. In the same way that the worship team rehearses every week, so should you. You have to pay the price for a good message, and part of that price is taking your teaching for a test-drive before you stand in front of your people on Sunday. We'll discuss the message run-through in detail in the next chapter.

We recognized that the niche we were best suited to reach in Berkeley were Cal students who were open to Jesus but unwilling to accept American church culture, who insisted on the diversity that has come to characterize the university. This meant that music would have to be central to our strategy and that we would have two poles—teaching and worship. We hoped that after students were attracted to Sunday morning, they might be convinced to stay and try out the community. So we called a recent Cal grad, an excellent musician, as our worship pastor. He and I have gotten together every week without fail to talk, pray, and plan. The result of this is that he has my trust and backing in whatever new thing he tries on Sunday morning. Our congregation has cutting-edge worship but also values the teaching I bring. Plus, we've recently started working a full year ahead by means of the preaching calendar, which frees up the worship pastor to plan further out.

Allan Collister, Church Planter and Lead Pastor
New Church Berkeley, Berkeley, California

Testimony

After preaching and music, testimonies are the single most powerful tool you can include in your worship service. People tune in to stories of life change, especially when they recognize some aspect of themselves in the story. It's one thing for you to get up and teach a biblical principle, but it is quite another for a person your listeners have been sitting with in the pews to stand up and share how God has used that truth in her life. You can incorporate testimonies into your service in three ways:

1. Have someone share a live testimony before the message.
2. Bring someone to the stage halfway through the message. This works especially well if the testimony illustrates a particular teaching point.
3. Shoot a video testimony in advance and show it at some point during the service.

There are many advantages to recording a testimony ahead of time. First, the person giving the testimony won't have to be available all day on Sunday if you have more than one service. This increases the number of people in your church who will be willing to give a testimony. Also, a testifier will often have an easier time telling his story on camera rather than in front of a live crowd. For example, not long ago, a gentleman in our church who had once tried to commit suicide came to us with his testimony. We knew it was something our people needed to hear, but we couldn't ask him to tell such an emotional story at all four of our Sunday services. So we arranged a time to film him talking about his experience in the comfort of his own living room. Then we had an editor edit the material down to a powerful four-minute video testimony that we showed in all four services. The impact was incredible.

When you decide to go with live testimonies instead of video, do so strategically. If the day's message is on the importance of small groups, ask one of your most relatable small group leaders to give a testimony. Ask her weeks in advance so she can come prepared. You may even want to have her write out her story and share it with a staff pastor first. The testimonies you incorporate are meant to serve a specific purpose. If you are in a smaller church, don't be tempted to give the platform to anyone who feels like sharing. That will create confusion, burn your time with your people, and probably scare any unbelievers in your crowd to death. Small groups provide the perfect environment where people can share. But on Sunday mornings, keep things simple and well planned. (To see an example of a recent video testimony at The Journey, visit www.ChurchLeaderInsights .com/Engage.)

Recognizable Media

The entertainment industry is an undeniable power player in our culture. Your attenders and mine spend hours on media every week. They watch television. They go to movies. They listen to music. They read magazine articles about celebrities. So harking back to the theme of riding culture's rails rather than forging a new path, you can capitalize on this cultural reality to get your point across.

The best form of recognizable media to incorporate into a service is a well-known movie clip. When you use a movie clip that supports or illustrates a point in your message, you create a bridge between yourself and your listener—a bridge that your message can walk across. People immediately connect with characters they recognize. If Clark Griswold pops up on the big screen in your service, people will chuckle before they even see the clip. They will feel a connection thanks to their own past experience with Chevy Chase's iconic films. That connection can work wonders for your message. (For information on securing film clip permissions, visit www.ChurchLeaderInsights .com/Engage.)

Remember that using well-known movies—rather than independent movies, niche movies, or your mom's favorite movie—is key. People need to immediately recognize and relate to what's on the screen. Sometimes you can get away with using less-well-known films if the clip perfectly supports the point you are making and if you are willing to take a few minutes to introduce the clip. But in general it's best not to stray too far off the beaten blockbuster path.

A note of warning: don't ever use media just for the sake of using media. If it doesn't illustrate your point or move the big idea of the sermon along, nix it. Media can be extremely powerful when applied well, but fizzles if your goal is simply to be cool. (For a list of resources we use at The Journey to find and utilize recognizable media, visit www.ChurchLeader Insights.com/Engage.)

Original Media

Original media is anything you produce in-house. Be as creative as you want with your original media. If you have talented audio/video people in your church, ask them to get involved. You could shoot a series of videos to illustrate various points in an upcoming message series. You could do man-on-the-street interviews within your church or within the community on a specific topic. For example, when we were ramping up to kick off a message series on prayer called "Vertical," we spent a couple of Sundays doing man-on-the-street interviews with people in our church. Our media team would simply stop people before or after the service and ask them (on camera) how they felt about prayer or what questions they had about prayer. Then we edited their responses into a short video piece that we played as an introduction to our series. (To see an example of a man-on-the-street video used at The Journey, visit www.ChurchLeader Insights.com/Engage.)

Another thing we do at The Journey is tape our baptism celebrations and then edit them down into a jam-packed, three-minute baptism video to show in the Sunday services. (To watch one of our baptism videos, go to www.ChurchLeader Insights.com/Engage.) Be open to anything that may help your people grasp what God is doing around them and what he wants to teach them. Original media takes more work than recognizable media does, but when done well, it can be extremely influential.

If you don't feel you are capable of creating original media well, don't do it at all. If you don't have anyone in your church who knows how to direct, edit, and shoot video—and if you aren't in a position to hire anyone—you may want to stay away from this element. Creating poor original media will hurt you much more than you think.

Drama

The best dramas create a tension that the teaching pastor gets to resolve with the message. During the "Vertical" series, we started one of the messages by having an actor alone onstage, engaging in a conversation with God. He was asking questions like, "God, why do you want me to pray if you already know what I need? What's the deal with me having to voice it to you?

Do you just want to hear me beg?" The tension building in the room was palpable. People began to get a little uncomfortable. When the actor stepped offstage—leaving those questions hanging in the air—the teaching pastor came in with the message and addressed them. Like original media, drama is difficult to do well, but it can be extremely powerful.

Everything Else

You have the freedom in your services to be as creative as God leads you to be. Reflect his creativity. Think outside the box. If you can think of a creative element that can be well executed and that moves the service forward, do it. If you have a sculptor in your church, have her sculpt onstage during your message to illustrate your main point. Use poetry or dance. God has put talented people in your path for a reason. Make every effort to find a way to use them. Just understand the priority of what you are doing.

> *Being sixty-two years of age and always trying to stay on the cutting edge of ministry, I knew I needed assistance to reach a younger generation. I must say that through these systems, I have learned more than at any other time in my ministry. Thanks to the worship planning system, our worship team has a new understanding of the importance of being prepared for a service since everything we do has eternal value. The Thursday midnight rule has been beneficial to me, but I have also stressed its importance among all our leaders who are teaching on Sunday. It is a simple thing but when followed makes Saturday night and Sunday morning a whole lot better. The future is bright, and still after forty years of pastoral ministry, I am excited, challenged, and eager to make a difference in the lives of others. These things will*

go a long way toward bringing good health to our church. When the church is healthy, it will grow.

Gerry Carnes, Senior Pastor
Marietta First Church of the
Nazarene, Marietta, Georgia

Elemental Excellence

Planning produces possibilities. There are some life-transforming moments your church will experience only if you are willing to do the work of creative, advance planning. Another powerful, creative moment worth mentioning took place during the "Relationship Rescue" series I referred to earlier. On the Sunday I was teaching on divorce, Jason had a drama planned. The piece focused on a married couple. As the drama unfolded, the husband found out that his wife had been having an emotional affair with another man. You could feel the anxiety rising in the room. The drama left our congregation on the edge of their seats. As the lights went down, our worship team took the stage with a song that was currently at the top of the pop charts: "How to Save a Life" by the Fray. Our dance team accompanied the song, their movements bringing a sense of redemption to the emotional roller coaster the congregation had just experienced.

This eight-minute glimpse into the reality of a couple on the verge of divorce required weeks of preparation, three of our worship arts teams, dozens of volunteers, and impeccable timing within the service. But it was more than worth the effort. Without the key elements of the worship planning system we've discussed here (the preaching calendar, the series planning meeting, and the like), that great moment in our service would not have been possible. It's only when we give the Spirit time to speak, and our teams time to listen and work, that we are able to experience such life-transforming moments in our services.

When people walk through your doors on a Sunday morning, they want to be inspired. They want to be stirred, thrilled, and called to a higher level of living. As church leaders, our job is to do everything we can to make that happen. We have an obligation to utilize every tool available to us that may cause our listeners to become more like Jesus, that may help his truth to resonate in a new way. We don't have to trudge through the same routine week after week. Our services don't all need to look like the one before. God has given us the freedom to engage with him creatively in order to show the various facets of his greatness to the people he brings our way. As long as we are honoring him and glorifying his name, there are no rules. Remember: Sunday matters. Do what it takes to align the elements for excellence.

8

the trial run

Conducting a Message Run-Through

What we hope ever to do with ease, we must learn first to do with diligence.

Samuel Johnson

Work at telling others the Good News, and fully carry out the ministry God has given you.

2 Timothy 4:5

One of the first rules actors learn is to speak the words of a script out loud before they go into an audition room. Why? Because no matter how many times they run through their part in their head, no matter how well they've committed it to memory, no matter how clearly they can see their delivery in their mind's eye, they understand this truth: things sound differently when spoken aloud.

Every good actor knows that if the audition room is the first place that the words of a script leave his lips, he's doomed. He should have already spoken them in the hallway or the bathroom or wherever he can find space to do a trial run. His ears need to hear his voice say the material before it matters most. Though you and I are not performers, the same rule applies. Your message should not leave your lips for the first time on a Sunday morning. If it does, you will have missed an incredible opportunity to strengthen your delivery and your overall craft.

If any of you speak at conferences or do guest speaking at other churches, you probably already know the power of taking your message for a trial run—even if you don't realize it. When I began teaching in venues other than The Journey, I noticed something interesting. I had figured out that I didn't need to prepare a fresh message every time I spoke. Instead, I would teach a message that I had already taught on a Sunday morning. Oddly, I started noticing that I did a better job when I preached outside my church. After a few of these experiences, I figured out what was going on: I had already practiced delivering the message. I had taken it for a test flight. And it always sounded better the second time around than it had the first. The secondhand listeners were getting better teaching than my own church's attenders. Without even meaning to, I had made my preaching more effective.

One of my mantras has become, "Never preach a message once." And preaching it at multiple services during the same weekend doesn't count. Your first service is not your trial run. If you want to increase the value of your preaching, you must develop the habit of pre-preaching—that is, preaching your message ahead of time, gathering feedback, and integrating the changes into your notes for Sunday. At minimum, put yourself in the room with an audio recorder or a video camera. Better yet, gather some interested, trusted staff members to listen and give you feedback. What exactly does this look like? The process for conducting a message run-through is shown below.

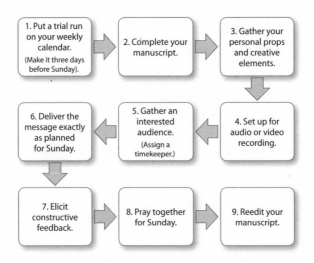

Most of these steps are self-explanatory, but here's a quick breakdown.

1. *Put a trial run on your weekly calendar.* I suggest making this a standing appointment in your calendar. Just like your worship team rehearses at the same time every week, you should have a set weekly time for your message run-through. Schedule your run-through for at least three days before Sunday so you will have time to make necessary adjustments.

2. *Complete your manuscript.* Your manuscript needs to be completed at least three days before the upcoming Sunday. You can't do your run-through without a completed message.

3. *Gather your personal props and creative elements.* If you are going to use props or creative elements in your message, use them in your trial run. You don't want any surprises on Sunday. For example, during a past message on the oneness of marriage, I took two pieces of construction paper—one orange and one purple—and a stick of Elmer's glue onstage with me. A few minutes into the message, I glued the two pieces of paper together to illustrate what happens when we get married. Then I set the paper to the side to dry. Toward the end of my message, I discussed the tragedy of divorce and how two people who have been joined by God can never separate completely. To illustrate, I tried to pull those two pieces of paper apart. They wouldn't come apart cleanly. Streaks of purple were left on the orange paper and vice versa. There is no way I would have used that illustration onstage without first testing it out in my sermon run-through.

4. *Set up for audio or video recording.* When was the last time you watched yourself on video or listened to yourself on audio? You should take part in this humbling exercise every week. We all have quirks and habits we aren't aware of. I had a speech impediment growing up, so there are certain words I have to work really hard to say. Sometimes I have awkward pauses before those words. When I take the time to listen to myself on audio or watch myself on video, I am more aware of those tendencies and better able to correct them. Learn to be your own best critic and strive for greater excellence every week. (To learn more about conducting a message run-through, download my free ebook titled *How to Double the Impact of Your Preaching* at www.ChurchLeaderInsights.com/Engage.)

5. *Gather an interested audience.* Gather your worship pastor and other members of your staff to sit in on your run-through. Assign someone to be the timekeeper. The best-case scenario is to deliver your message to a small group of people who have the service's best interests in mind and are able to give you good feedback. But if you can't pull anyone together, don't let that keep you from doing a run-through. Just deliver your message to an "Audience of One." Let it be a time between you and God. Ultimately, you are not reliant on anyone other than him.

6. *Deliver the message exactly as planned for Sunday.* Even if you make a mistake, lose a thought, or forget something, continue to treat the trial run as if you were in front of a live audience. Don't interrupt your flow to give commentary or explain yourself to your team. For example, don't step out of the moment to say something like, "When I get to this point, I'm going to . . ." Teach as if it's a Sunday morning. That's the only way to get an honest assessment of how clear your message is.

On that note, if it's at all possible, do your message run-through in the same location you'll be teaching in on Sunday. If you don't have access to your weekend location, re-create it to the best of your ability in your run-through space. If you usually preach with a stool beside you, put a stool beside you. If you have a table that you place your notes on, bring a similar table to the run-through. Pay attention to details and make your run-through feel as much like Sunday as possible. This may feel weird the first few times you do it, but it will pay off. Believe me.

7. *Elicit constructive feedback.* The feedback you get through this process can make your message infinitely stronger. You will see how your illustrations hit the listeners. They can tell

you if something isn't translating clearly. They may suggest you reorder a point or two. You may be surprised how emotionally difficult this step can be. You will likely be tempted to argue or defend yourself, but resist the urge. Feedback from others who have your best interests in mind will do nothing but make you a better communicator. (For more on the importance of feedback, see chapter 10.)

8. *Pray together for Sunday*. Don't forget that the true power of transformation on Sunday comes from God. Ask for his blessing on the entire service. Pray for those attending to be open to the Word of God. And be sure to pray for yourself as well.

9. *Reedit your manuscript*. Ernest Hemingway once said, "There is no such thing as a great writer. There are only great re-writers." Sit down after your run-through and put in the hard work of rewriting what needs to be rewritten. Tweak what needs to be tweaked. Consider all the feedback you received and move ahead accordingly. You don't have to make all the changes your listeners recommended. You can be the judge—but be honest and prayerful as you take the bench. To keep your timelines on track, make sure you have your renewed manuscript finalized by the deadline you've set for yourself.

Consider the life of an Olympic boxer. To those of us looking on, his entire world seems to be defined by the few minutes he spends inside the ring. In reality, those few minutes are simply a reflection of his life every other day of the week. His personal commitment to training and preparation determines his success or failure. Everything he does leading up to the moment he steps through the ropes shapes the outcome of the fight. In the same way, the moment you step onstage or into the pulpit to preach God's Word is a critical moment. Your commitment to training and preparation will determine how well it goes. You need to make sure you've done everything you can to ensure success because, in this case, success isn't a fancy belt—it's RTLs.

The responsibility you and I have to bring God's Word to his people is too great for us ever to get comfortable. We should always be pressing toward improvement. The only way we are going to get better—and the only way our messages are going to

> *Excellence is doing the best you can with what you've been given.*

be as strong as they can be week to week—is to commit to a regular trial run. Excellence is doing the best you can with what you've been given. Conducting a weekly message run-through is a step in the direction of practicing excellence intentionally.

> *I have been impacted by the challenge to do a message run-through, which we call the "Pre-Preach." At first, this was difficult for me, because somehow I thought I'd let out my steam if I preached my message ahead of time. It sounds silly now, but that's where I was. Now, we have a regular "Pre-Preach" every Wednesday at 2:00 p.m. We are actually two weeks ahead, which give worship, media, and creative teams more time to prepare. I can't imagine going back; this is one of the most freeing things we do.*

Donald Ross, Lead Pastor
Creekside Church, Mountlake Terrace, Washington

9

defining relationships

The Pastor/Worship Pastor Challenge

You must have role clarity, or you will have role confusion. If left unfixed, role confusion soon becomes role conflict.

Pat MacMillan

But our bodies have many parts, and God has put each part just where he wants it. . . . The eye can never say to the hand, "I don't need you." The head can't say to the feet, "I don't need you."

1 Corinthians 12:18, 21

Remember the story I told you earlier about my first experience as a pastor working with a worship leader? While comical, the scenario I encountered is all too common. This weekend, in churches across America, teaching pastors and worship pastors will stand in front of rooms full of churchgoers and take turns doing their own thing. If the songs the worship pastor has chosen for the day happen to be along the same thematic lines as the message the teaching pastor preaches, the two pastors will high-five after the service and revel in how powerfully the Holy Spirit moved. If the teaching pastor preaches on something diametrically opposed to the songs the worship pastor chose, they will mark it up to God's indiscernible will and hope for better the next week. In most cases, these pastors will lock the church doors and head to Sunday lunch having no idea that their relationship with one another is key to being able to cooperate with the Holy Spirit in planning cohesive, engaging worship services.

The nature of the pastor/worship pastor relationship is complex, to say the least. On the one hand, it is the most important relationship that exists on your church staff. Your respective areas comprise the two halves of an important whole. You share the stage, the message, and the creative elements of the service. You are both integral to creating a welcoming, engaging environment that will lead to RTLs. You are partners with each other and with God. When the relationship is working well, you have the privilege of seeing incredible fruit come from your joined efforts. But all too often a dark side lurks in crevices of the pastor/worship pastor connection.

While this relationship is the most critical relationship that exists in the church, it is also the relationship that carries the most potential for tension and stress. Small issues can easily go unaddressed. Misunderstandings fester. Expectations are not always met. Frustrations rise, and the relationship becomes strained. In fact, tense relationships between pastors and worship pastors are so common in American churches that they have become cliché. I'm sure you've heard plenty of jokes on the topic. Have you heard this one?

> Q: How many pastors and worship pastors does it take to change a lightbulb?
>
> A: Ten! One worship pastor to change the bulb and nine pastors to say, "You could have done it better!"

We make light of the common problems we have with one another for two reasons. First of all, we have a hard time putting our finger on exactly what causes them. Second—and as a result of the first—we don't know how to solve them. (For additional material on the pastor/worship pastor relationship paradox, download the free *Overcoming the Seven Challenges of a Worship Pastor* ebook at www. ChurchLeaderInsights.com/Engage.)

Over the years, both Jason and I have had many pastors and worship pastors tell us, "My relationship with my [pastor/worship pastor] may not be great, but we manage. It doesn't affect what we do on Sundays." I hate to shatter your illusion, but relational problems between the pastor and the worship pastor always affect the church's worship services. If the relationship is wounded, the people in the seats will notice some limping.

> *An Ineffective Pastor/Worship Pastor Relationship Leads To:*
>
> · *frustration*
> · *misplaced expectations*
> · *lack of clarity about worship services*
> · *poor worship services*
> · *incongruence on place of creativity in worship services*
> · *damaged trust*
> · *loss of friendship*

Good or bad, the details of this relationship play themselves out in our worship planning. And since effective worship planning is the key to being able to conduct life-transforming worship services, the results can be devastating—on an eternal scale. When the pastor/worship pastor relationship is ineffective, the church misses out on its full redemptive potential.

The worship planning system is the base structure that produces the services our people see. When miscommunication, confusion, frustration, and unmet expectations are chipping away at the base, it is going to suffer some damage. If the base is damaged, the tip isn't quite so glorious. So if we ever hope to have God-filled, life-transforming worship services week after week, we have to get this relationship straightened out once and for all. We have to figure out how we can work together most effectively. But first we have to identify where we are before we can get where we want to go. Most pastor/worship pastor relationships fall into one of four categories. Broadly, these relationships are:

> *When the pastor/ worship pastor relationship is ineffective, the church misses out on its full redemptive potential.*

1. Actively disengaged. You do your thing; he does his thing.
2. Passively disengaged. You want to see something fresh and new happen in your relationship and worship services, but you just don't have the time/system/structure for it.
3. Passively engaged. You may have a few connecting points in place and a strong desire to work together more effectively, but there's no real structure for moving forward.

4. Actively engaged. You and your pastor/worship pastor are fully engaged with each other and willing to put in the hard work of planning, implementing, and evaluating your worship services as a cohesive unit with a common vision. This is the ideal scenario for optimal worship planning.

Take a look at the details of the chart below. Which quadrant does your current situation fall into?

Quadrant 1: Actively Disengaged	Quadrant 2: Passively Disengaged
You do your thing, I'll do mine. Little to no collaboration on message and creative elements. Three songs and the sermon. Done. Let's keep things the way they are. Little value on using creative arts in the worship service. No communication about Sunday service preparation or postservice debrief. Unsure of what the message will be about this week.	Desire for effective services, but no planning structure. Some thematic connection between message and music/arts. Not against creative expressions, but no time or resources to implement them. Little communication about Sunday service preparation or postservice debrief. Unsure of what the message will be about next week.
Quadrant 3: Passively Engaged	**Quadrant 4: Actively Engaged**
Implementing some creative elements but with difficulty. Favorable opinion of using creative arts. Theme for Sunday service may be established, but specific elements are not clear. Some communication about Sunday service preparation and postservice debrief, but not very consistent or strategic. General idea of what the message will be about for the next two to three weeks.	High value on creativity and the arts in worship services. Pastor and worship pastor very hands-on in planning entire service (not just their parts). Structures for advanced planning in place. Both pastor and worship pastor give and receive feedback. High-level ownership of the service. Messages for the next four to six weeks well thought out.

What's your quadrant? How are you and your pastor/worship pastor doing in terms of this type of framing? Are you getting along well but know your ability to produce great services is being thwarted by a lack of systems? Do you feel like you are in one quadrant and he is in another? Are you at odds with each other? If you are stuck in quadrants 1 or 2, who is to blame? (To learn more about how to move toward quadrant 4, download the "Winning at the Pastor/Worship Pastor Relationship" audio resource at www.ChurchLeaderInsights.com/Engage.)

The Blame Game

Often, when relationships or circumstances aren't going the way we want them to, we jump into the traps of blame and denial. We deny that we are at fault in the breakdown, and we blame the other person for the issues that exist. In the pastor/worship pastor relationship, it becomes easy to pin the responsibility for every problem on our counterpart. Have you ever been guilty of the blame game?

Worship pastor, do you ever utter the phrase "if only" in regard to your pastor? Have you ever thought, "If only he would get his act together, then I could . . ." Pastor, have you ever thought, "If only our worship pastor would come through with this, then we could . . ." or "If only he could be more creative like the guy at the church down the street . . ."? Do you ever pass the buck? Have you ever thought, "That's his job, not mine" or "I wish he would get his act together so we could do something new"? Even if your relationship with your pastor/worship pastor is strong, you've probably thought something along these lines at one time or another.

Early on in ministry, I learned that the only person I have control over is me, and that's probably a good thing! If I had control over my wife, we would always eat at the restaurants I like and go to

Clint Eastwood movies. But I don't. So we talk, there's give-and-take, and we make the best decisions for both of us. Here's a news flash: I don't have control over my worship pastor either—and he doesn't have control over me. The same is true in your church.

Worship pastor, you can't say to your pastor, "Give me the message notes for the next five years, pronto!" Pastor, you can't say, "I know it's only two days before the service, but here's what I'm teaching. Go pick out the music and find a testimony and three video clips that will work with the message. And make it awesome!" Worship planning doesn't work that way. The key to winning in the pastor/worship pastor relationship is to succeed in the role you play as a part of the team. You have to constantly do the best you can to prepare, communicate, and support your pastor/worship pastor by excelling in your own responsibilities. (To learn more about the role of the worship pastor, download "The Call of a Worship Leader" audio resource at www.ChurchLeaderInsights.com/Engage.)

We all want our services to be powerful and God-inspired. We all want to have a good working relationship—even friendship—with our pastor or worship pastor. But a lack of communication is undermining our good intentions. One of the primary causes of tension in this relationship is unarticulated and unmet expectations. We don't understand what the other wants, and we have a difficult time communicating what we want. Neither party gets the other's vision for the worship services. We approach Sunday with competing ideas for how the day should play out. In our frustration, we pull back from one another, and as a result, we end up operating in quadrant 1 or quadrant 2. We resort to thinking in terms of "my part of the service" and "his part of the service" rather than looking at the service as a whole.

So how can you overcome the pastor/worship pastor challenge? How can you move past the resentment and uncertainty caused by miscommunication and unmet expectations? The answer exists in four straightforward steps. While all these steps are simple, they are not necessarily easy. But as you learn to take them, you will discover the fruit and joy of operating consistently in quadrant 4—of being actively engaged with one another and working productively toward a shared vision.

Scott walks into the kitchen area of FCC's office, thinking back through the testimony he and the team just shot. As he opens the refrigerator and reaches in for a bottle of water, he hears Tim come in behind him.

"Hey, how'd it go?" asks Tim.

Scott closes the refrigerator and sits down at the small round table. "They were a little nervous at first, but they calmed down as we got into it. Their story is so powerful. It's going to cut together well."

"Good! Yeah, that's one of the reasons I like video testimonies so much. People may get nervous in front of the camera, but they have time to work out their nerves and really tell the story. Live, their nerves sometimes get the best of them." Tim walks over to the counter and grabs a banana. "Want one?"

"Nope, I'm good, thanks. So I was reading the paper yesterday, and I came across an article that I thought you might be able to use in the Easter series kickoff message. I'll bring it in tomorrow."

"Great! Thanks, Scott."

"Absolutely. You never know, it may resonate with someone. I'll bring it; you can be the judge," says Scott.

"Sounds good. I'd love to see it. Hey, what was it you wanted to connect on this afternoon?"

"Oh, I just wanted to give you a quick heads-up that we are making a last-minute change in the dance for Sunday. We were going to do it during the third song of the worship set, but I'm going to move that song and the dance to the end of the service instead. I've been feeling like it would be a more powerful way to wrap things up. How does that sound to you?"

"So you are adding another song to replace the third song in the set?" asks Tim.

"Yep, I was actually just charting it out for the team."

"That works for me. You're right, the dance would be a strong ending note. Thanks for letting me know," says Tim.

"No problem. I always want to let you know about any changes as soon as they pop up." Scott takes another swig of his water and chuckles. "Well, guess this took the place of me stopping by your office. Gotta love impromptu water cooler meetings."

"Yeah, maybe we should move all our meetings to the kitchen. It's where I do my best thinking," Tim jokes. "So I'll see you at the message run-through this afternoon?"

"I'll be there, stopwatch ready," Scott says.

"Perfect. See you in a little while," Tim says. He tosses his banana peel into the trash can and heads back to his office.

Four Steps to Active Engagement

1. Cultivate Commitment

You and your pastor/worship pastor are a team. You need to own that reality and make an intentional decision to be committed to one another. Commitment really comes down to a combination of loyalty and trust.

Loyalty + Trust = Commitment

Loyalty. Worship pastor, do you carry the flag for your pastor? Do you speak well of him? Pastor, are you loyal to your worship pastor? Do you encourage and support him in any way you can? God has called both of you to your church and to your current relationship. The more loyal you are to one another, the stronger that relationship will be.

Support each other's vision. Worship pastor, be on board with the overall vision God has given your pastor for the church. God has called you to be led by your pastor, so don't undermine that calling by skirting the vision or holding negative opinions of him. Try to see things from his perspective. Pastor, you've been put with your worship pastor for a reason. He is integral to the mission God has given your church, so stick by him. Build him up and help him succeed. This is a two-way street; be loyal to one another.

Trust. One of the most important things you can give your pastor/worship pastor is the assurance that you are leading your area of ministry with excellence. Worship pastor, show your pastor that you are growing and taking risks. Do what you say you are going to do. When he sees you doing your job well, that develops trust. Pastor, the same goes for you. When you make a commitment to your worship pastor, follow through. Give him what he needs to do his job well. As you both handle yourselves with excellence in your area, loyalty develops, trust grows, and commitment happens.

2. *Clarify Roles*

The majority of relational tension and worship planning trouble can be averted by clearly defining your roles and the expectations inherent in those roles. Most conflict happens when something doesn't get done or doesn't get done in the way the other party expected. Clear roles and defined expectations act as the grease that keeps the pastor/worship pastor relationship turning without friction. Think through these questions:

- What is your role in the pastor/worship pastor relationship? What is your counterpart's role in the relationship?
- Do you have a clear job description? Does he?
- What do you need to do every week to get ready for Sunday?
- How do you measure the effectiveness of your role?

One of the most practical things you can do to keep your relationship healthy is to make a list of what you think is expected of you every week in order to get ready for the service. Ask your pastor/worship pastor to do the same. Then arrange a time to sit down together and talk through those lists. Make sure you both have clearly defined expectations for yourself and that you each know what you can expect from the other.

Once you know what is expected of you, you can measure your own effectiveness by setting deadlines for each item on your list. If you know it is your responsibility to get the message notes to your worship pastor by a specific time on a specific day, set that as a hard deadline for yourself and take note of how well you hit the deadline each week. A culture of punctuality is one of the requirements of an effective worship planning system. When both the pastor and the worship pastor have a list of things they know they need to do and self-imposed deadlines to keep them on track, things immediately begin operating more smoothly. (To learn more about expectations for both the pastor and the worship pastor, visit www.ChurchLeaderInsights.com/Engage.)

3. Communicate

In his book *The Performance Factor: Unlocking the Secrets of Teamwork* (a book I highly recommend, by the way), Pat MacMillan writes, "The biggest problem with communication is the assumption that it has taken place."[5] Can you relate? I know I can. Communication is tricky. Just think about how often you communicate something to another person only to realize later that the message they received was not the message you intended to send. People hear and interpret our words through their own set of filters, which means they often hear something different from what we thought we said. That's why we can never assume communication; we have to assure communication. The best way to assure communication is to adhere to the Principle of Overcommunication.

> *The Principle of Overcommunication means you go over and above to make sure what you've communicated has been received correctly.*

The Principle of Overcommunication means you go over and above to make sure what you've communicated has been received correctly.

What does that look like practically? When you sit down with someone on your staff to explain a project, ask them to repeat back to you their understanding of what you've just said. Get in the habit of asking people to repeat deadlines you've given them or details of assignments you've given them. As you learn to hear how your people hear you, communication will become clearer. Also, keep these communication buzzwords in mind:

- Open: create environments that allow a free flow of communication.
- Initial: don't wait for someone else to talk to you first. Be quick to share problems, thoughts, changes, etc., with the necessary parties.
- Intentional: overcommunication doesn't just happen; it requires an active mind-set.
- Honest: give and receive input honestly. Ask for help when you need it. Be an open book.

An open flow of communication between the pastor and the worship pastor is essential to creating a coherent worship planning system. The teaching pastor should be ready, able, and willing to speak into the worship pastor's area, and vice versa. The worship pastor and his team can help the pastor invent creative moments in the message; the pastor can speak ideas and suggestions into the creative area. Open communication paves the way for shared vision and synergy.

4. Create Systems

Good intentions give way to old habits if there aren't any systems to hold them in place. To ensure that the pastor/worship pastor relationship stays on track and stays strong, buffer it with systemic support.

1. Set the preaching calendar. As we saw in part 2, the preaching calendar is the lynchpin of your worship planning

system. It gives you and your pastor/worship pastor common ground to build on.

2. Establish a meeting culture. Schedule your series planning meeting and your weekly worship planning meeting, and then stick to the time slots you've given them. Don't underestimate the importance of these meetings; they are the rudders on your worship planning ship.

3. Determine deadlines. You should have deadlines throughout the week leading up to Sunday, with the final deadline being the Thursday midnight rule (or your own variation of the Thursday midnight rule).

4. Evaluate after every service. No service is finished until the pastor and worship pastor have evaluated it. Evaluating each service is key to keeping this relationship actively engaged. It is also the best way to make sure every weekend is better than the last. We'll discuss service evaluation in detail in part 4.

Actively engaged pastor/worship pastor relationships don't happen by default. Rather, they involve the coming together of two individuals who are dedicated to personal excellence and mutual respect and who are willing to do whatever it takes to create worship services that lead to radically transformed lives. When the pastor and worship pastor are both committed to excelling in the roles they play as part of the team, the Holy Spirit will be able to move with amazing frequency, and RTLs will abound. (To learn more about how to invest in your worship leader, download "Three Ways to Help Your Worship Leader Succeed" at www.ChurchLeaderInsights.com /Engage.)

Prior to implementing the worship planning system, burning the midnight oil on Saturday night was all too common for my creative team and me. In fact, I wouldn't even characterize us as a "team" at the time. My modus operandi back then was to function week to week in isolation as I prepared the Sunday sermon. Undoubtedly, I would come up with a creative idea on Friday afternoon for the weekend message. Since a couple of the guys running the PowerPoint or helping with the worship team really loved our church, they would work with me into the wee hours of the morning trying to edit a video or prepare a special song for the end of the message. But I noticed their frustration with my "fly by the seat of my pants" leadership style, especially when things didn't turn out as well as they could've on Sunday if they would have had more time to prepare. Personally, I was frustrated and flat out exhausted by the constant pressure of developing sermons and creative elements at the last minute. After learning and implementing the worship planning system, we now have an approach to the weekend that has never been more fun, creative, and effective. We've actually established a creative worship arts team and an annual preaching calendar. Now, instead of working week to week, the team works in advance on song selection, stage decor, and creative elements such as dance, video testimonies, and more. As a result, I now look forward to each weekend at Pocono Community Church. We celebrate the success of our team, which designs and executes a compelling presentation of the gospel of Jesus each and every week.

David Crosby, Lead Pastor
Pocono Community Church,
Mount Pocono, Pennsylvania

PART 4

evaluating
and improving
worship services

10

evaluating for excellence

The Philosophy behind Service Evaluation

Feedback is the Breakfast of Champions.

Rick Tate

To learn, you must love discipline;
it is stupid to hate correction.

Proverbs 12:1

How do you feel when someone offers you advice concerning your worship service? Does something inside you rise up in indignation—"Hey, buddy, I've been doing this a long time; I don't need your input"—or are you able to take in what you are hearing, sift it for truth, and keep what can be helpful to you? I don't know about you, but I have never liked feedback very much. If I had to guess, I bet you don't either—

in your flesh, anyway. Let's face it, we are by nature prideful people. We are also insecure people. Our temperature rises a little when someone starts to tell us what we may have done wrong or how we could improve the thing we've already put so much time and effort into. We would rather have people stroke our egos, tell us how engaging and inspirational we are, and revel in our ability to hit the ball out of the park every Sunday. (C'mon, you know it's true.) Unfortunately, there's a pesky little proverb that flies in the face of this attitude. Proverbs 12:1 tells us, "To learn, you must love discipline; it is stupid to hate correction." Drat.

As if that proverb weren't enough to convict us, Paul addresses our condition in more detail with a lesson in humility. He writes:

> Don't be selfish; don't try to impress others. Be humble, thinking of others as better than yourselves. Don't look out only for your own interests, but take an interest in others, too. You must have the same attitude that Christ Jesus had. Though he was God, he did not think of equality with God as something to cling to. Instead, he gave up his divine privileges; he took the humble position of a slave and was born as a human being. When he appeared in human form, he humbled himself in obedience to God and died a criminal's death on a cross. (Phil. 2:3–8)

Paul's words are particularly piercing for those of us who are pastors and worship pastors. When it comes to our worship services, many of us have a hard time being humble. We know that God has called us to our position, and we have heard from God in our planning, so we don't really care to hear other people's opinions on how we can do things better. We have been given the authority. Surely we know what's best, right?

Consider this: Jesus was the very Son of God, but he didn't hold his head high with pride. He didn't dismiss the input of others, even though he knew everything (and he actually *did* know everything). Rather, he humbled himself. He thought of others more highly than himself. He didn't need to be right; he just needed to fulfill the purpose and plan God had for him on this earth. Jesus's example of humility is a perfect representation of how we need to approach evaluation and feedback concerning our worship services. A prideful heart will only keep us from seeking out and hearing input that can improve our services exponentially. But a heart of humility and a spirit that loves discipline and correction will allow us to create a culture of feedback that has the potential to take our churches to the next level.

Keeping Score

Even though we may initially struggle with receiving it, we can't deny the importance of feedback. I know you have goals you want to accomplish for your church, just as I do. If you didn't, you would have stopped reading this book long ago. But you are still with me because you have a desire to plan your worship in a way that leads to engaging, life-changing services. If you and I ever hope to reach the goals we have set for ourselves and our churches, we have to be open to evaluating the progress we are making—and we have to have a system in place to foster that evaluation.

Without measurements, we have no way to know how we are doing; we have no way of keeping score. Let's say you decide to sit down for a little Monday Night Football. You turn the television on, and the game is already underway. What's the first thing you look for? The score, right? But what if the score isn't there? What if the heads of the NFL decided they were going to have teams play each other every week, but they weren't going to assess which teams were doing better than others? Maybe some of the owners and coaches got together and decided they didn't like keeping score; they would rather just operate on how things felt week to week. I know I wouldn't sit and watch two teams run up and down the field, throw a ball, and tackle each other if there was no evaluation mechanism in place. You wouldn't either.

> *There is no excellence without evaluation.*

Why is it, then, that we think we can spend months putting together a Sunday service and then, after the final amen, close the book on that service without evaluating how things went? As I've stated many times, one of our primary responsibilities is to reflect God's excellence to the world, starting with the people in our churches. But here's an underlying principle of that truth: there is no excellence without evaluation.

If our goal is to be excellent every Sunday, we need to find a way to evaluate our services so we can see what needs to be tweaked and continually move toward improvement. Excellence happens through making small improvements week by week—improvements that can be made only as we are open to honest evaluation and feedback about the service. That means we have to learn to love correction and discipline; otherwise, according to Proverbs, we are stupid—and that isn't good for anybody.

Excellence, for our purposes, is doing the best you can with what you've been given. To achieve excellence, you have to commit to aiming for the highest level of impact you can possibly reach—the highest level of impact God would have you reach. Believe me, God's dream for your church is much bigger than your dream. When you begin to grasp what he would like to do in and through your ministry, humility will inevitably follow and so will the willingness to do whatever it takes to fulfill his plan and purposes for you.

The first step to being able to evaluate effectively is to pinpoint a specific goal. A good goal is something that is better than your best but still believable. While being excellent is a goal in itself, we need to be more precise for evaluation purposes. A worthy goal to aim for each week is to try to look like a church twice your size. If you are a church of 65, what would it take to look like a church of 130? If you are a church of 500, what steps could you take to look like a church of 1,000? How will you know if you are making the right moves toward improvement and growth? Here are some questions to consider:

- If your church were twice its current size, what would you change about your preparation? In what ways would you prepare differently for Sunday?
- If your church were twice its current size, what would you change about your leadership structure? What would your staff look like?
- If your church were twice its current size, what would you change about your communication? What steps would you take toward clarity?
- If your church were twice its current size, what would you change about your systems? What new systems would you need to put in place?

155

The purpose of these questions is to get you thinking about leading into the future—about setting a goal that is both precise and higher than your current level of operation. Don't structure for where you are; structure for where you want to be. (For resources on breaking through your next barrier to growth, go to www.ChurchLeaderInsights.com/Engage.)

> *As a result of our extra effort in worship preparation, we're finding that people are more ready to invite their unchurched friends to church. They know that even though they have taken a relational risk in inviting, their friends will clearly hear the gospel presented in a way that's understandable, creative, compelling, and applicable to everyday life.*
>
> Andrew Thompson, Pastor
> Columbia Grove Covenant Church,
> East Wenatchee, Washington

In his great volume *Leading at a Higher Level*, Ken Blanchard writes, "To move toward goals, people need feedback on their performance. . . . Can you imagine training for the Olympics with no one telling you how fast you ran or how high you jumped? The idea seems ludicrous, yet many people operate in a vacuum in organizations, not knowing how well they are doing their jobs."[6] How well you do at looking like a church twice your size—with twice as many members, twice as great a facility, twice as many first-time guests, twice as many new believers, and ultimately twice as many RTLs—will let you and your staff know how well you are doing your job. Stretching yourself to this level isn't going to happen overnight; it is going to take week-by-week dedication to constant and never-ending improvement, otherwise known as the CANEI Principle.

Tim pulls into the parking lot of the diner, thinking about how quickly time flies. Seems like he and David just had a breakfast meeting, but already another month is gone. He thinks to himself that it's no wonder pastors get so discouraged. You turn around and another week is barreling down on you. Tim sends up a prayer of gratitude that God has helped him break out of that crazy cycle.

David knocks on Tim's car window, jolting him out of his reverie. Tim turns off the engine and hops out of the car.

"Hey, man," Tim says. "You caught me in another world. I was just thinking through some stuff."

"No problem," David says. The two men head into the diner, and David continues, "I've been so excited about our meeting today. I have something I want to show you."

The host seats Tim and David in their usual booth. As soon as they order coffee, David begins rummaging around in his bag. He pulls out a yellow notepad. Tim smiles to himself when he sees "Preaching Calendar" written across the top.

"My team and I sat down last week and talked through the preaching calendar for all of next year. We couldn't get away for a retreat, but we are definitely going to do that next year. It's already on the calendar!" David pushes the notepad toward Tim as he continues talking. "There are a couple of gaps, but for the most part, we know what we are doing, at least thematically—and several of the series titles are already nailed down. I feel so good about this. God was definitely leading the process."

"David, this is great! I had no idea you were going to take the step so quickly."

"Well, like you said, this calendar is the base for everything. And next year is coming down the track fast. I didn't want to spend another year caught in the week-to-week cycle. I can already see how our services are going to be so much better—and how I am going to be less stressed." David chuckles. "My wife loves the concept, by the way."

The waitress comes by and fills the coffee cups. David continues, "I feel like I just want to keep learning. This is a whole new way to think about worship planning. I can't even imagine what God is going to do through this. I have been operating way beneath what he's called me to. Putting this whole system in place is going to take everything to a new level."

"God is into systems, that's for sure," Tim says. "And he loves it when they help us reflect his nature. Good stuff, David! I'm excited for you. You're right. You'll be operating at a new level from here on out."

After they order their breakfast, Tim decides to move ahead with David. Since he is grasping things so quickly and obviously has a newfound passion for planning powerful worship services, Tim doesn't want to hold anything back. No need to take it slowly.

"So, David, there's a lot to worship planning. The preaching calendar is a major piece of it, but there are also timelines to be set for your series planning and Sunday planning."

"Yep," David jumps in. "We've started working on those."

"Great. You are on the ball," Tim answers. "There's another piece that I think is going to be really helpful to you. Have you ever heard of the principle of CANEI?"

"The principle of CANEI?" repeats David. "No, I don't think so. What does CANEI mean?"

"CANEI is an acronym that stands for constant and never-ending improvement. If you really want your services to soar, you have to commit to CANEI. You can never be satisfied with what you did last week, even if it was a great week. Always keep moving forward; always be working to reveal God's excellence in a new, more powerful way."

"Wow. CANEI. I like it," David says. "Makes sense. Of course the services should get better. I mean, I should be letting God call me higher every week, right? So, how? How do I know what needs to be improved upon each week?"

"That's the key question. The only way you can follow the principle of CANEI is to set up a system for feedback, listen to the feedback with humility, and then make the changes that need to be made for the next week. Every week your service will get a little better than the week before. Just imagine, after a year of small, weekly improvements, your service will be head and shoulders above where it is now. But if you aren't evaluating every service, it will just keep moving along the same track."

"Okay," David says, "so how do I go about it? How do I create a culture of feedback? Who evaluates my services? And when?"

Tim smiles at David's eagerness. "Let's talk it out. Mind if I borrow the notepad for a minute?"

David passes the pad and a pen to Tim, takes a gulp of his coffee, and leans in a little closer.

Creating a culture of feedback is essential to the principle of CANEI. You can't strive for constant and never-ending improvement if you can't put your finger on what needs improving. You have to know the score. You have to know what's going right and

evaluating and improving worship services

what's going wrong. How else will you be able to make the changes necessary to look like a church twice your size? A culture of feedback starts with you. You set the stage, so to speak, by designing an environment in which feedback and evaluation are welcome, encouraged, and appreciated. You can do this in several ways:

- *Plan a time for feedback.* Rather than just expecting your team and key leaders to approach you with any feedback they may have regarding the service, plan a specific time to engage them in conversation. Schedule a meeting within two days of every service. (We will discuss this meeting in detail in the next chapter.)

- *Begin with prayer.* When you pull your team together to evaluate the service, always begin with prayer. Thank God for everything he has done through the service, thank him for meeting you there, and ask him to open your eyes to what you can improve for his glory.

- *Be grateful for feedback.* Over the years, I have learned to be extremely grateful for feedback. If I'm doing something wrong, I want to know it. The fact is, if one of my staff notices something out of whack in the service, then several people in the congregation probably notice it too. The same is true for you. Rather than repeating the same mistake next week, be grateful that someone speaks up and gives you the opportunity to fix whatever is wrong. Well-received feedback leads to improvement, so why wouldn't you be grateful for it?

- *Be your toughest critic.* When I walk into a debriefing meeting, I like to be the first one to lay out the mistakes I know I made during the service. I highly recommend getting into the habit of being your own toughest critic.

160

When the people around you see that you want to admit and address areas that need improvement, they are more likely to be open with you.

- *Give and get specific feedback.* Don't let vague comments slide. They won't do you any good. If someone tells you that your sermon on Sunday didn't really connect, ask him to be more specific. What exactly didn't connect? Was it a specific story that was confusing? Was it the way the points were ordered? Make sure you get and give feedback that is specific. If it's not specific, it won't be helpful. (For more on giving and receiving feedback, visit www.ChurchLeader Insights.com/Engage.)

- *Focus on the issue, not the person.* When you are giving feedback to someone, focus on the problem at hand without putting the person involved on the spot. When mistakes happen or problems surface, the people involved usually feel terrible already. There is no need to place blame. Simply focus on what needs to be fixed for the next Sunday. Around The Journey, we always say, "You can make mistakes every Sunday, as long as they are new mistakes." The problem comes when the same mistakes are made over and over. You don't want people to be hesitant to try new things because they are afraid to fail. Failing forward is part of improvement. Focusing on issues rather than on people creates an environment in which staff members and volunteers are open to feedback—good or bad.

- *Ensure action for each point of feedback.* Getting feedback isn't enough; you have to take action on each point of feedback. If you don't, nothing changes. (Again, more on the nuts and bolts of this in the next chapter.)

- *Seek feedback as a way to honor God.* When your motivation for giving and receiving feedback is right—that is, when you are truly trying to honor God through the process—you can't go wrong. Your team members will be able to discern your heart. If you approach feedback humbly and with a desire to grow toward excellence, they will likely approach it the same way. Then you can move together toward honoring God more fully each week.

Even though our natural tendency may be to push back from feedback, we will learn to love it as we grow into the leaders God has called us to be. Like Jesus, we are to be servant leaders—leaders who are humble in heart, always concerned more with the advancement of the kingdom than with ourselves, and willing to put in the hard work that leads to constant and never-ending improvement. In *Leading at a Higher Level*, Blanchard goes on to say:

> Called leaders have servant hearts, and they love feedback. They know the only reason they are leading is to serve, and if anybody has any suggestions on how they can serve better, they want to hear them. They look at feedback as a gift. When they receive feedback, their first response is, "Thank you. That's really helpful. Can you tell me more?"[7]

Imagine the changes that would occur in your church if you were able to fully embrace the heart of a servant leader. You can get there by practicing humility, learning to love discipline, and putting a system in place for eliciting the feedback you want and need. God can cultivate the heart within you if you'll let him. You can choose to love correction and commit to using it to grow the kingdom. As for the system, just keep reading.

162

11

closing the book

How to Evaluate and Improve Your Services

I know of no more encouraging fact than the unquestioning
ability of a man to evaluate his life by a conscious endeavor.

Henry David Thoreau

The way of a fool is right in his own eyes,
but a wise man is he who listens to counsel.

Proverbs 12:15 NASB

I once had a friend, Harold, who was a master builder. When
Harold built houses, they were built to last. He didn't cut
corners; he pursued excellence at every turn. Now Harold has
gone to be with the Lord, but many happy people continue
to call the houses he built "home." These homeowners rave
about how their houses are cool in the summer and warm in

the winter. Their basements don't flood when heavy rains come, unlike some of the other houses nearby. What makes Harold's houses so much better than the neighbors' houses? One simple thing: Harold understood the value of evaluation and improvement. With every house he built, he learned a lesson that made the next house better. As experience built on experience, each successive house became stronger and more exceptional than the one before it. Harold paid meticulous attention to detail, constantly asked himself what he could be doing better, and then followed through on the answers. He recognized that there is no excellence without evaluation.

Building your worship planning system is a little like building a house. Your preaching calendar lays the foundation. Your message series time lines and specific Sunday time lines frame up the walls. Your message run-through, creative element integration, and active engagement with your pastor/worship pastor are the Sheetrock. But something has to solidify the structure; something has to ensure that it is protected from the elements and grows more livable with each passing year. Enter evaluation. Evaluation acts as the mortar that holds together everything you have built. Without it, your structure exists, but it teeters and creeks. It has some misalignments and gaps that never get fixed because they go unnoticed—until the heavy rains come and the basement leaks. That's when you realize that if only you had been evaluating your work and making improvements along the way, your results would have been much more exceptional.

The final piece of the worship planning system is the process for evaluating and improving your services. The only way your service is going to be better next week is if you evaluate what happened this week. As we learned in the last chapter, we can't move forward without feedback. There is no excellence without evaluation. Now that you understand what it takes to construct every other area of your worship planning system, let's look at the glue that holds it all together. There are four key steps to evaluating and improving your worship services.

Step #1: Take Notes

As you ramp up to Sunday, you should already be in evaluation mode. You should be evaluating every step of your worship planning process and the result it is producing. One of the best ways to integrate evaluation into your overall mind-set is to get in the habit of constantly jotting down notes on what is working and what needs improvement. As you go through the week, keep a couple of note cards in your pocket and think thoughts of evaluation at every stage of preparation. In your preplanning, ask yourself, "How is this going to come across? How is the end result going to look?" Evaluate your message run-through. Ask yourself, "What went well? What needs to change?" Evaluate rehearsal. Evaluate how things go during your setup for Sunday. Jot down a quick note when you see something that needs improvement. Pale ink is better than the best memory.

> ### When Should You Evaluate?
>
> · *in preplanning*
> · *in the message run-through*
> · *during rehearsal*
> · *during setup/ Sunday rehearsal*
> · *between services*
> · *after each Sunday*
> · *after each series*

Most importantly, make sure you have your note cards with you on Sunday morning. While evaluation throughout the week is essential, Sunday evaluation is critical. Sunday is game day. It's the day that needs the most attention. Train yourself, your pastor/worship pastor, and any key staff members to take notes when something stands out both during and immediately following the service. For example, if you see a rough transition, note it. If you don't have a note card with you for some reason, write it on a bulletin. Or if you know something didn't come across the way you wanted it to during the message, make a note. If one of your PowerPoint slides or a graphic image didn't come up like it should have, you know what to do.

If you conduct multiple services on a Sunday, each successive service should be better than the one before it thanks to your team's eye toward evaluation. At The Journey, we have four services every Sunday—three in the morning and one in the evening. After each service, we spend about ten minutes shaking hands and saying hello to everyone, then we gather our key people together in the back to talk through any changes that need to be made before the next service based on the notes we've all jotted down. Whatever can be fixed on the fly, we fix before the next service. As you can imagine, the 6:30 p.m. service is always our best service of the day because we've been making small improvements at every interval leading up to it.

Step #2: Conduct a Meeting to Debrief the Service

Here's something that may surprise you: your service doesn't end when your people are dismissed. The book isn't closed on any Sunday service until you have debriefed it with your team. One of my colleagues, Kerrick Thomas, played college football. When we first started holding meetings to debrief the service, he used to tell me how much they reminded him of the "game tape" meetings his team would have after each Saturday's game. In the day or two after every matchup, the coach would sit the team down to watch the game tape. They would dissect every missed tackle, every flubbed pass, and every route that was run incorrectly. Whether the team had won or lost didn't matter. They always studied the tape so they would know what needed improvement before the next game. Then they would work to fix those things during the week.

If football teams understand the importance of debriefing each game in order to be better the next week, shouldn't we? As church leaders, we should never dream of walking into a new Sunday without having dissected the last Sunday's service to see what went right, what went wrong, and where we can improve. These football players are playing a game; it has no eternal value. We, on the other hand, are dealing with people's lives and destinies. Doesn't it make sense that we would give what we do on Sundays the same—or hopefully, better—attention and evaluation that the guys chasing a pigskin up and down a field do?

The debriefing meeting is our chance to go over the game tape each week. I suggest conducting this meeting by the end of the Tuesday following your service. (On a side note, we also hold a meeting at the end of every series to discuss what we could have done better from a series planning perspective.) For an effective meeting, everyone needs to show up with his or her notes from the service and the previous week. Attendees need to show up prepared. Once underway, the meeting doesn't have to be long and drawn out. We usually like to keep ours to thirty minutes. In fact, we have even made this a Monday lunch meeting in the past. We meet in my office, order some takeout, and spend a few minutes putting feedback on a whiteboard. What exactly goes on the board? Glad you asked.

Step #3: Ask Four Feedback Questions

You should ask four questions in your meeting each week. These questions—which allow for open and honest feedback—will tell you everything you need to know to improve next week's services. They are:

1. What went right?
2. What went wrong?
3. What was missing?
4. What was confusing?

If you have a whiteboard or a large sheet of paper, write, "What went right?" at the top. Start your meeting by going over all the good things that happened on Sunday. Your people need to be able to give positive feedback rather than focusing exclusively on what needs to be fixed. Otherwise, you run the danger of creating a culture of critique. Make this list as long as possible, and then take a few minutes to pray and thank God for what he did on Sunday.

After you cover what went right, ask the next three questions at the same time: What went wrong? What was missing? What was confusing? Some people will be quick to tell you what went wrong, but others won't. They'll be more comfortable telling you what was missing or what may have been confusing. Asking people what was missing and confusing is a subtle way to draw out wrongs that need to be addressed. All three questions are really just three ways of getting to the issue of what needs to be fixed. Take a look at this example from one of our recent meetings.

Sunday, April 2

What Went Right?

- New arrangement of seats in the auditorium made for a better audience experience
- Pancakes for breakfast backstage (yum!)
- New stage extension helped teaching pastors feel closer to the congregation
- Video testimony worked well in the message
- Video teaching at the 6:30 p.m. service went smoothly
- New camera in the balcony added some great shots
- Placement of coffee and donuts in the lobby made for a better entry flow
- Lighting on painting was not dark like the last time we had painters during the service
- Good debrief session after 10:00 a.m. service
- Abby (new DJ) did well after 10:00 a.m. service
- Fill-ins stayed up longer on PowerPoint as was discussed in last week's meeting
- Moment of silence to respond at the end of the message worked well
- Good lighting on new stage extension
- Nelson walking around on the stage extension had a good feel
- Dance
- Steve: new sound guy
- Worship order flow
- Setups for transitions: video testimony, etc.

What Went Wrong?

- Joanie too loud and too early reading verse at 10:00 a.m. service (JH/JC)
- Angle of the right side camera—too far to the right
- Jason's wireless guitar pack didn't work at 11:30 a.m. service (JH)
- Assistant stage managers moved too slowly onstage and offstage (JH)
- Assistant stage managers didn't wear black (JH)
- Pastor five minutes over in every service
- The seating of the congregation was not right at 6:30 p.m. (SW)
- Houselights went up too slowly after the video at 10:00 a.m. service (JC)
- Music between services was too loud (JC)
- Camera shots during worship were not always on the person leading/most active (JC/JH)
- No roving camera at 10:00 a.m. service
- Bass head fell off during the worship set at 11:30 service (check for damage this week and repair if necessary) (RF/JH)

What Was Missing?

- No house music after 6:30 p.m. service (JC)
- No "meet the pastors at back" announcement at 10:00 a.m. service (CB)
- Pastor's wireless mic pack was "missing" but really at the stage manager's table (create list of responsibilities for stage manager and assistant stage managers) (JH)
- Memory verse cards were not printed and available (JHK)
- Not everyone was onstage at 9:00 a.m. for prayer time (JH)

What Was Confusing?

- Should we have put up lyrics for song "40"? (JH/JC)
- Offering at 10:00 a.m. service went very slowly (SW/CB)
- Assistant stage managers didn't know where to stand when offstage—always in the way (JH)
- Stage manager didn't meet assistant stage managers until way into the service (JH)
- Joanie didn't seat the audience after the first worship set (JH)
- Clapping on slower song—some team members were, others were not (JH)
- First worship set—too new? (JH)

When we ask these four questions, we get a glimpse into our service from several perspectives at once. (Download a free service evaluation worksheet at www.ChurchLeaderInsights.com/Engage.) The ensuing improvements can be invaluable. But to turn the evaluation list into actual improvement, you have to take the next step.

Step #4: Assign Individual Follow-up

Once you have your evaluation list written on the board, the next step is to assign every wrong, missing, and confusing item to an individual for follow-up. If you look at the example above, you'll notice that each item has a set of initials next to it. The person who is assigned to an issue is held accountable for making sure the issue is corrected or addressed in such a way that it won't be a problem at the next service. Jason and I are responsible for following up during the week with people who have a point assigned to them to make sure everything is on track.

Your ability to address each point during the week will depend in part on your current staffing structure. When staff members are assigned to the line items, the level of accountability should be extremely high. One week should be more than enough time to right the wrongs. If, however, you rely on the help of volunteers, you'll need to give them more time. Some items may hang around a little longer than one week. At The Journey, most of the points are now assigned to paid staff people, so if the same item shows up on the board two or three weeks in a row, there's a problem. Again, new mistakes are okay, but we aren't going to allow the same mistakes to happen again and again. A culture of excellence—and the peer pressure it produces by default—is a powerful motivator.

Just think about the change that the four questions and assigned action points could bring to your church. Even if you correct only 10 percent of the problems you write on the board, your service will be 10 percent better next Sunday than it was this Sunday. Over time, those small 10 percent improvements lead to a complete overhaul in the seamlessness, power, and impact of your services. But if you do not evaluate and take specific steps toward improvement, you won't move any closer to excellence than you are right now.

Every Monday night in staff meetings, we evaluate every aspect of the Sunday morning services. We call our evaluation the "What Went." Using the evaluation strategies of the worship planning system, we have been able to evaluate each service effectively and correct many mistakes. We evaluate what went right, what went wrong, what was missing, and what was confusing. Before implementing the system, we would just get frustrated with aspects of our Sunday morning worship experience. After implementing the "What Went," we find it a lot easier to make adjustments before the next Sunday morning, which provides a greater worship experience the following week and beyond. Constant evaluation has helped us create a better atmosphere. We have found that with evaluated experience, guests and regular attenders have a better worship experience that turns into life change.

Rob Huffman, Pastor
Clearview Church, Virginia Beach, Virginia

As Harold learned with his houses, relentless evaluation and consistent, incremental improvements add up to greater excellence at every turn. When you commit to this proven four-step process for evaluating and improving your worship services, you are committing to partnering with God to create a more powerful, more engaging environment each week—an environment in which the Holy Spirit is free to move mightily and in which lives will be radically transformed.

David pulls out of the diner parking lot, thinking through the day's breakfast discussion. As he drives, he ponders all the points Tim has laid out in the last few months about planning life-transforming worship. He feels like a sleepwalker who is just waking up to the reality of his partnership with God and the potential for his church.

David is happy with his progress so far, but he knows there's a lot left to learn and a lot left to do—starting with putting a note card in his pocket and a debriefing meeting on the calendar for next Monday. Turning the corner toward the church, his mind moves to Sarah, his worship pastor. David realizes he needs to take the active engagement concept seriously and make sure they are on the same page. She was on board with the preaching calendar and starting the timelines, but maybe their interaction still isn't quite what it needs to be to create the best services possible.

David pulls into his church's parking lot, whips into his usual space, and turns off the car. He sits in the silence, quietly thanking God for moving in his church and for giving him the insight to be a better steward of the time he has been given.

A knock on the car window startles David out of his thoughts. As he looks up, Sarah gives a little wave. David jumps out of the car.

"Hey, Sarah!" David says. "You caught me deep in thought."

"Are you just coming back from your breakfast with Tim?" Sarah asks.

"I am," David answers. "As a matter of fact, he's given me a lot for us to talk about. Do you have a few minutes? I'd love to run some of this by you while it's still fresh."

"Sure thing," Sarah says. "Meet you in your office in ten minutes?"

"Great. See you in a few. I think you are going to be really excited about all I've got to share. It's life-transforming stuff."

conclusion

Five Steps to More Engaging Worship Next Sunday

If you keep on doing what you've always done,
you'll keep on getting what you've always got.

W. L. Bateman

Commit your actions to the LORD,
  and your plans will succeed.

Proverbs 16:3

Sunday matters. What you and I do week in and week out
is of eternal significance. Even though we may get frustrated at times, we can never forget that we are handling holy
responsibilities. Take a look at these words from the psalmist:

I waited patiently for the LORD to help me,
  and he turned to me and heard my cry.
He lifted me out of the pit of despair,
  out of the mud and the mire.

> He set my feet on solid ground
>> and steadied me as I walked along.
> He has given me a new song to sing,
>> a hymn of praise to our God.
> Many will see what he has done and be amazed.
>> They will put their trust in the LORD. (Ps. 40:1–3)

We have the awesome privilege of partnering with God in his work of lifting people out of the pit of despair and placing their feet on solid ground. How could we give him anything less than our best effort? How could we opt to operate out of stress, lack, and confusion rather than plans, peace, and power? When you and I wrap our minds around the unparalleled responsibility that rests on our shoulders, we will be willing to do whatever we can to cooperate fully with God and his purposes.

The Big Rocks

You've probably heard about the professor who walked into his classroom one day with an empty jar. In fact, if you've read either *Ignite: How to Spark Immediate Growth in Your Church* (Baker, 2009) or *Maximize: How to Develop Extravagant Givers in Your Church* (Baker, 2010), I know you've heard it, because I tell the story in both. It bears repeating and examining from the perspective of all we've discovered about worship planning.

Once there was a wise professor who set out to prove a point to a bunch of sleepy students. One morning, he walked into his classroom with a big, widemouthed jar under his arm. He made his way to the front of the room and set the jar on his desk. With the students paying little attention, he filled the jar with five big rocks. He put the rocks in one by one until the jar couldn't hold any more. Then he asked his students, "Is this jar full?" They half-nodded their assertion that it was.

The professor pulled a bucket of pebbles from under his desk. Slowly, he poured the pebbles into the jar. They bounced and settled into the small spaces that had been created between the rocks. Once again, the professor asked his students, who were now slightly more awake, "Is this jar full?" They all quietly contended that, yes, of course it was.

The professor proceeded to pull another bucket from beneath his desk—this one filled with fine sand. As the students looked on, he tilted the bucket of sand, and the granules quickly filled in the barely visible cracks and crevices left between the rocks and pebbles. This time when asked, "Is this jar full?" the class answered with a resounding, "Yes!"

In response to his students' certainty, the professor reached under his desk and brought out a pitcher of water. The students watched in amazement as the professor poured the entire pitcher into the jar.

Now the professor asked a different question: "What was the point of this illustration? What was I trying to teach you through this now-full jar?"

A student in the back called out, "You were showing us that you can always fit more things into your life if you really work at it."

"No," replied the professor. "The point is that you have to put the big rocks in first, or you'll never get them in."

If the professor had tried to put the big rocks in last, they never would have fit. But since he made the rocks his priority, everything else was able to settle into place accordingly. When it comes to your worship planning system, there are five big rocks you need to put in place as quickly as possible. Once you get them in the jar, the rest of the system will fill in the empty spaces and gaps around them. If you can't do everything suggested in these pages right away, focus on getting the big rocks set. Without them, nothing else we've discussed will be useful, but with them, you will be light-years ahead of where you are now. Here are the five big rocks and what you can do this week to start getting them into position.

Rock 1: Long-Term Mentality

Immediate Action Step: start breaking the week-to-week mentality by asking yourself what you can do today to start planning for the next two to three weeks. Then do it.

Rock 2: Preaching Calendar

Immediate Action Step: sit down with your calendar, look over the next year, and ask God to begin guiding you in planning for his purposes.

Rock 3: Pastor/Worship Pastor Relationship

Immediate Action Step: proactively connect with your pastor/worship pastor and get his input on how things are shaping up for next Sunday.

Rock 4: Message Run-Through

Immediate Action Step: put a message run-through on your calendar. Invite your worship pastor and other key staff to attend.

Rock 5: Evaluation

Immediate Action Step: Put a note card in your pocket and make a note when you see something that needs improvement.

Encourage your worship pastor and other key staff members to do the same. Schedule a meeting for the Monday or Tuesday after your upcoming services to debrief.

Speaking of filling in the space around the big rocks, let me give you a little jump start. Here are a few pebbles that can help you close some small gaps right away. Take a look at these five little things that can make a big difference in your services next Sunday. Combined with the action steps mentioned above, they will give you a quick start toward conducting more engaging services:

1. *Give clear directions.* Make sure your worship pastor says, "Let's pray!" before beginning a prayer. New people— especially unchurched people—don't know what is expected in an unfamiliar environment. Failing to give them clear direction can cause them to feel like outsiders, like they don't know the code. The same rule applies to having people sit and stand. Clarity is key in this context too. Whenever possible, give your people clear directions.

2. *Shorten the greet time.* Seventy percent of the people sitting in your seats are introverts; they are intimidated by the greet time. The greet time can also be extremely awkward for new people—especially when everyone else seems to know each other. Allow enough time for people to shake one or two hands and then ask them to be seated. (Remember, give clear directions.)

3. *Don't put anyone on the spot.* While you may think it looks spontaneous, putting someone on the spot in your service tells everyone you weren't prepared. Don't call for an impromptu testimony if your service is running too

short. Don't ask someone to pray if you haven't asked him in advance. Have a plan and stick to it.

4. *Open with the hook.* Kick off your message with the most interesting thing you have to say. Hook your listeners with the first four or five minutes. People remember how you begin and end the message. Don't save your witty intro story until after the Scripture or the review of last week's teaching. Lead with the hook.

5. *End big.* Leave your people with something that will make them feel great about their experience at church that day. Use fun, relevant wrap-up music. Keep things upbeat. Make them smile. In short, make sure your people hit the street on a high note.

Put these five little things into practice now as you work toward placing your big rocks and getting your worship planning system on track. As we've seen before, little things can make a big difference.

In Closing

My charge to you is twofold. First, put the five big rocks in place and then, through the guidance of the Holy Spirit and the help of this book, begin proactively filling in around them with the details of the worship planning system. Your system won't come together overnight, but if you commit to doing your part of the work, God will lend his power to your effort and it will take shape more quickly than you may think.

Second, take the immediate action steps I've suggested. Don't hesitate. Do the small things you can do this week to get the worship planning ball rolling. If you do a message run-through this week, your message will be stronger for it. If you make an extra effort to connect with your pastor/worship pastor, you'll see the fruit right away. You don't have to wait until your preaching calendar is in place to put a note card in your pocket. Implement the five little things that can make a big difference. Do what you can do now to be more effective this week, next week, and the week after.

Proverbs 16:3 tells us that if we commit our work to the Lord, we will succeed. In the case of your worship planning system, success is measured in terms of RTLs—radically transformed lives—that have been touched and changed by the power of the Holy Spirit working through the earthly details of your worship services. As you put the worship planning system in place, you will be doing your part to engage and change the eternity of every person who walks through the doors of your church. What a responsibility; what a calling. May we never take it lightly.

acknowledgments

Nelson Searcy: My eternal gratitude to Jesus Christ for the opportunity I have each week to lead people toward true worship.

In addition, I would like to thank the following pastors and leaders for influencing my views and shaping my thoughts on creativity, healthy systems, and worship planning: Rick Warren, Steve Stroope, Milton A. Hollifield Jr., Steve Ivey, Dan Southerland, Wayne Cordeiro, Bill Hybels, Bryant Wright, and Elmer Towns.

I must also express a huge thanks to my colleagues at The Journey Church, both past and present. Since 2001, I have had the privilege of being the dumbest person on an extremely smart team. Kerrick Thomas and Jason Hatley, in particular, have shaped the thoughts in this book. To the current staff, I love doing church with you! To those whom God will call to our staff in the future, I'm waiting to hear from you!

Although mentioned above, I must highlight my friend and colleague Jason Hatley. Since 1997, in one form or another,

I have been either onstage with Jason or backstage planning worship services with him. I can't think of a better brother in arms when it comes to the topic presented in this book. Simply put, there would be no worship planning system without him. In addition to being a worship pastor par excellence, Jason is a dedicated follower of Jesus, a husband, and a father. No wonder God has blessed his local church leadership and his ministry to other worship leaders.

Jennifer Dykes Henson has been a partner on my last six nationally and internationally published books and a trusted colleague on many other projects. She continues to step up her game with each new opportunity. Her skills as a writer, editor, and interpreter are hard to overstate (if you think I exaggerate, you should see how pathetic my ramblings are before she adds her magic touch). Thank you again! And just in case this is your first book with me, you should know that everyone's favorite characters, Jon, Liz, Pastor Tim, and now Pastor David, would not exist without Jen's creative mind. As members at The Journey, Jennifer and her husband, Brian, serve as true models of fully developing followers of Jesus.

My sincere appreciation to the team that makes Church Leader Insights happen every day and every week. You have no idea how significant your impact is on pastors around the world. Thank you, Scott Whitaker, Tommy Duke, Cristina Fowler, and Jimmy Britt.

I must also express my thanks to the now one thousand-plus pastors who have completed one of my Senior Pastors Coaching Networks. Many of the ideas shared in these pages were first beta tested on you. Your feedback, improvements, and insights have made this a much stronger book. Thank you for living out the "learn and return" principle. A special thanks to those alumni who shared their testimonies in this book.

This is my third book with the tremendously dedicated people at Baker. My thanks to Chad Allen, Jack Kuhatschek, Rod Jantzen, Brooke Nolen, Adam Ferguson, and all the fine people at Baker Publishing who have made this book infinitely stronger than it was when I submitted the original manuscript. Thanks for your commitment to my ramblings.

Finally, I must thank the love of my life, Kelley, and my son, Alexander. Our family went through several major transitions during the completion of this book, including sending our son to school, moving to a new home, and undergoing an unexpected emergency room visit and subsequent (successful) surgery on yours truly. All the while I kept sneaking away to write, and Kelley and Alexander kept supporting me. Kelley, your love and support continue to amaze me. I say it in every book, but it's true: I love you now more than ever! Alexander, who will turn five years old just prior to the release of this book, is just now learning that what he gets to do in Kids Church is quite different from what we do in Big Church. May God give us the grace to teach him to be a true worshiper. Tonight I asked him if I could include him in this book, and, in only the way a little child can, he said, "Maybe not this one. The next one, Daddy." Alex, I'm including you anyway because it's just one expression of my love for you. Thank you both for your commitment to this book and your continual support.

Jason Hatley: Above all, my deepest gratitude to Jesus Christ, who saved me for his purpose and gives me the strength and passion to live that out every day in serving the church.

I would also like to thank the men and women who have given me not only inspiration but also the opportunity to discover and teach the lessons of this book.

To Nancy Beach, thank you for your friendship and for taking a chance on letting me teach these principles at the Willow Creek Arts Conference for so many years.

To Rick Muchow, who gave me my first opportunity to invest in worship leaders in the early years of our church.

Likewise, I would like to thank Milton A. Hollifield Jr. and Steve Ivey for giving me a stage to develop my gifts on.

To James Forrest, Jeff Clark, and David Snider, thank you for your friendship and partnership in creating music, leading worship, and having some "glory days" to look back on with enjoyment.

To Jimmy Britt, who gave me a church to lead worship in and a glimpse into what starting a new church could be like.

To the pastors and staff of The Journey Church, every Sunday we serve together is an honor and a privilege. I would specifically like to thank Nelson Searcy and Kerrick Thomas, who modeled for me as a young worship pastor what it meant to love and serve the local church.

To The Journey's Worship Arts Team, thank you for your partnership in creating life-transforming worship services every week at The Journey. Without you, our church would not be what it is. Thank you for allowing God to work through you in such a powerful way.

A very heartfelt thanks to Nelson Searcy. Nelson took a chance on me when I was nineteen years old. He saw potential that others did not. I am eternally grateful for the many years of service together since then. Your vision, but most importantly your personal investment, has helped shape me during the most significant years of my life and ministry. It is a pleasure to call you pastor, leader, and friend.

To my grandfather, James C. "Charlie" Hatley, for reminding me that if I kept "playing that guitar," it would take me somewhere.

To my brother, Adam Hatley, who helped me discover my call to ministry and has served as my hero for these many years.

To my father, Buddy Hatley, who believed so much in me as a young musician that he was willing to provide whatever I needed to sing and perform. More importantly, you taught me the value of family, work, and unconditional love.

To my mom, Nancy Hatley, who showed me the grace of walking with God and living a life of worship. I miss you, but I know you are experiencing true worship at the feet of Jesus every day.

To my wife, Karen, I love you with all my heart. There is no one I would have rather gone on this adventure with. Your love and support have strengthened and encouraged me, and I am so thankful that God showed me the great favor of allowing me to spend my life with you.

To my children, Abigail and Charlie, I pray every day that you will grow up to be worshipers, that you would give not only your hearts to Jesus but your very lives to his service. Thank you for helping me understand how much God loves me.

Jennifer Dykes Henson: Thanks first to God, who, in his wisdom and power, has given me the privilege of knowing and working with several thoughtful pastors who have understood the significance of creating engaging worship environments. While I won't call them all by name, I'd like to thank each and every one.

The one I will call by name is Nelson Searcy. Nelson, once again, thanks for your vision and your commitment to empowering the church, through its leaders, to reach its full redemptive potential. Partnering with you in this work is an honor I don't take for granted.

I'd also like to thank Jason Hatley for his insight and attention to detail in crafting these pages—and the system they contain.

Last but certainly not least, I want to thank my husband, Brian, without whom I couldn't imagine living the writer's life. Thanks for the laughter and love you bring to every day.

appendix

preaching calendar

January 1—"A New You for a New Year" (NS)

Life 360: Friendship, Finances, Faith, Freedom

January 8—"Life in Surround Sound" (KT)
January 15—"Faith: Broadband Beliefs" (NS)
January 22—"Finances: Next-Gen Management" (NS)
January 29—"Friendship: Wireless Connections" (NS/KT)
February 5—"Freedom: Life to the eXtreme" (KT) (Communion)

Roommates, Bad Dates, and Great Mates: Desperate Sex Lives—Season 2

February 12—"Sex . . . and It Was Good" (NS)

February 19—"Marriage: The Two Are United into One" (NS/KT) (Baby Dedication)

February 26—"Dating: Male and Female He Created Them" (KT)

March 5—"Temptation: The Fruit Looks So Fresh and Delicious" (KT/CB) (Baptism)

March 12—"Purity: Neither of Them Felt Any Shame" (NS)

Vertical (Prayer)

March 19—Sermon #1 (NS)

March 26—Sermon #2 (KT)

April 2—Sermon #3 (NS)

April 9—Sermon #4 (NS) (Communion)

TGIM: Thank God It's Monday!

April 16 (Easter Sunday)—Sermon #1 (NS/KT)

April 23—Sermon #2 (NS)

April 30—Sermon #3 (KT)

May 7—Sermon #4 (NS) (Baptism)

May 14—Sermon #5 (KT)

May 21—Sermon #6 (NS)

May 28 (Memorial Day Weekend)—Stand-alone message (NS/CB)

God on Film

June 4—Sermon #1: *Da Vinci Code* (NS)

June 11—Sermon #2 (KT/NS)

June 18—Sermon #3 (NS)

June 25—Sermon #4 (KT)

July 2—Sermon #5 (KT; maybe with NS)

July 9—Sermon #6 (NS)

July 16—Sermon #7 (NS/CB)

July 23—Sermon #8 (NS)

Saturday, July 29, Beach Baptism

Got Questions (or Guest Speakers)

July 30—Sermon #1 (NS/KT)

August 6—Sermon #2 (KT)

August 13—Sermon #3 (NS)

August 20—Sermon #4 (NS)

August 27—Sermon #5 (KT/CB)

September Series

September 3—Sermon #1 (NS)

September 10—Sermon #2 (NS)

September 17—Sermon #3 (KT) (Baptism)

September 24—Sermon #4 (NS)

Blueprint for Life

October 1—"The Purpose of Purpose/The Meaning of Life" (NS)

October 8—"To Infinity and Beyond" (NS/KT)

October 15—"I Think; I Can" (NS with KT/CB)

October 22—"My Spiritual Blueprint" (KT)

October 29—"My Physical Blueprint" (KT with NS/CB)

November 5—"My Financial Blueprint" (Baptism)

November 12—"My Career Blueprint"

November 19—"After Completing Blueprint for Life/Going the Distance"

Christmas Series

November 26—Sermon #1

December 3—Sermon #2

December 10—Sermon #3

December 17—Sermon #4

December 24—Christmas Eve (TBA)

You can download a free copy of The Journey's most current preaching calendar at www.ChurchLeaderInsights.com/Engage.

journey design calendar

- Set a deadline twenty-one to thirty days out for the final design of the message series postcard to go to print with drafts due on days 7, 14, and 18 (see timeline below).
- Day 7: Request two or three designs to look at on day 7. These designs will be reviewed by the lead pastor and the worship pastor for approval of one design. Once one design is selected, the designer/team will work on this design.
- Day 14: Draft 2 due.
- Day 18: Semifinal draft due.
- Day 20: Final proof and approval.
- Day 21: Final draft sent to printer.

Day 1	Day 2	Day 3	Day 4	Day 5	Day 6	Day 7
Designers given series title/sub-title to begin postcard design						Two or three design proposals due
Day 8	Day 9	Day 10	Day 11	Day 12	Day 13	Day 14
						Draft 2 due
Day 15	Day 16	Day 17	Day 18	Day 19	Day 20	Day 21
			Semifinal draft due		Final proof and approval	Final draft sent to printer

Here is an actual example from our "Vertical" series.

February 12—Begin design ideas for "Vertical."

18—Two or three design proposals due.

25—Draft 2 due (chosen design with initial edits and corrections).

March 1—Semifinal draft due.

3—Final proof and approval.

4—Send to printer (usually a two-day turnaround).

19—"Vertical" series kickoff.

three types of worship orders

Simple Worship Order

Preview video
Worship team—worship songs
   3–4 songs
Host—welcome/greet/connection card
Worship team—worship songs
   1–2 songs
Video roll-in
Teaching pastor—message/prayer/next steps
Possible video clip or testimony used during message
Host—Important information/offering

The worship leader controls the first half of the service, while the teaching pastor controls the second half of the service. For a downloadable version of this worship order, visit www.ChurchLeaderInsights.com/Engage.

Worship Order

Giving the people of Metro New York City the best opportunity to become full developing followers of Jesus...

Series: God on Film
Message: The Proposal
Finding Mr./Mrs. Right

Date: June 21, 2009
Location: Upper West/Village

				Sound Check
6:45			4:45	Setup Begins
8:00			5:15	Band Sound Check
8:55			6:00	Pastors' Sound Check
				- Table and Chair
				- Mic Check and PPT
9:10			6:10	Sunday Focus Time
9:15				**Cue to Cue**

CUE #					Service Begins
1	9:40	11:10	12:40	6:10	Pro Presenter Announcements
2	10:00	11:30	1:00	6:30	**Worship Team (16)**
					Everybody Praise the Lord - A (Jason)
					Let the Praises Ring - D (Jason)
					Everything That's Beautiful - D (Erin)
					Transition: Erin does Welcome/Greet; seats audience.
					Sweet Child of Mine - performance - A (Jason/Erin)
					Transition: Adam enters SL.
3	10:16	11:46	1:16	6:46	**VIDEO:** Father's Day Clip **(2)**
4	10:18	11:48	1:18	6:48	**AB:** Welcome **(4)**
5	10:22	11:52	1:22	6:52	**Worship Team (3)**
					Love the Lord - D (Erin)
					Transition: Erin seats audience.
6	10:25	11:55	1:25	6:55	**VIDEO:** Roll-in **(1)**
					Transition: Band, vox exit SL during video roll-in. Table, stool, and plasma enter.
7	10:26	11:56	1:26	6:56	**NS:** Message Part 1 **(35)**
8					**VIDEO: Man on the Street:** Relationship Interviews
9					**NS:** Message Part 2
10					**VIDEO:** Get Smart
11					**NS:** Message Part 3/Prayer/Next Steps
12	11:01	12:31	2:01	7:31	**AB:** Next Steps/Imp. Info /Offering **(4)**
13					**VIDEO:** Darryl Strawberry Promo **(1)**
14					**AB:** Wrap-up
					Service Ends
15	11:05	12:35	2:05	7:35	**Walkout Music:** Are You Gonna Be My Girl? (Jet)

Split Worship Order

Preview video
Worship team—worship songs
  2–3 songs
Host—welcome/greet/connection card
Video/drama/arts
Worship team—worship songs
  2 songs
Video roll-in
Teaching pastor—message (part 1)
Worship team—worship songs
  2 songs
Teaching pastor—message (part 2)/prayer/next steps
Host—Important information/offering

Control of the service begins with the worship leader, shifts to the teaching pastor, goes back to the worship leader, and finally rests with the teaching pastor. For a downloadable version of this worship order, visit www.ChurchLeaderInsights.com /Engage.

Salsa Worship Order

Preview video
Worship team—worship songs
  2–3 songs
Host—welcome/greet/connection card
Video roll-in
Teaching pastor—message (point 1)

Worship Order

Giving the people of Metro New York City the best opportunity to become full developing followers of Jesus...

Series: Revolve

Message: The Myth of Worship

Date: May 17, 2009

Location: Upper West/Village

					Sound Check
	6:45			4:45	Setup Begins
	8:00			5:15	Band Sound Check
	8:45				Drama Sound Check
	8:55			6:00	Pastors' Sound Check
					- Table and Chair
					- Mic Check and PPT
	9:10			6:10	Sunday Focus Time
	9:15				**Cue to Cue**
CUE #					Service Begins
1	9:40	11:10	12:40	6:10	Pro Presenter Announcements
2	10:00	11:30	1:00	6:30	**Worship Team (19)**
					Not to Us
					Let the Praises Ring
3					**Drama:** Scripture/Spoken Word
4					Revolve
					Made to Worship
					Transition: Erin does Welcome/Greet; seats audience.
5	10:19	11:49	1:19	6:49	**VIDEO:** Roll-in **(1)**
					Transition: Band. vox exit SL during video roll-in. Table. stool. and plasma enter.
6	10:20	11:50	1:20	6:50	**NS:** Message - Intro **(6)**
7	10:26	11:56	1:26	6:56	**JH:** Message - Point 1 **(5)**
8	10:31	12:01	1:31	7:01	**Worship Team w/ Possible Dance (3)**
					Heart of Worship - vocal and acoustic guitar only
					Transition: Erin seats the audience. Table, stool, and plasma return to stage.
9	10:34	12:04	1:34	7:04	**JH:** Message, Point 2 **(6)**
10	10:40	12:10	1:40	7:10	**NS:** Message, Point 3-4/Prayer **(11)**
11	10:51	12:21	1:51	7:21	**NS:** Next Steps/Connection Card **(4)**
12	10:55	12:25	1:55	7:25	**Worship Team (7)**
					O Praise Him
					Not to Us - reprise
					Transition: Erin seats the audience.
13	11:02	12:32	2:02	7:32	**NS (am)/JH (pm):** Next Steps/Imp. Info/Offering **(3)**
					Service Ends
14	11:05	12:35	2:05	7:35	**Music:** Today Is the Day (L. Brewster)

Worship team—worship songs

  2 songs

Teaching pastor—message (point 2)

Music/video/drama/arts

Teaching pastor—message (point 3)

Worship team—worship song

Host—Important information/offering

Controls rotates throughout the service. For a downloadable version of this worship order, visit www.ChurchLeaderInsights .com/Engage.

Worship Order

Giving the people of Metro New York City the best opportunity
to become full developing followers of Jesus.

Series: Christmas Traditions   **Date:** December 17, 2007
Message: The Tradition of Redemption   **Location:** Upper West / Village

CUE #				Sound Check	
	7:00			Setup Begins	
	8:00			Band Sound Check	4:45
	8:45			Drama/Dance Sound Check	
	9:00			Pastors' Sound Check	
				- Table and Chair	
				- Mic Check and PPT	
	9:10			Sunday Focus Time	
	9:15			**Cue to Cue**	
CUE #				**Service Begins**	
1	9:40	11:10	12:40	PowerPoint Announcements	6:10
2	9:57	11:27	12:57	**Video:** Deck the Halls (3)	6:27
3	10:00	11:30	1:00	**Worship Team (17)**	6:30
				Go Tell It on the Mountain - Jason (stand and sing at the end)	
				Hark the Herald Angels Sing - Ashley	
				Gloria - Jason & Ashley	
				O Come All Ye Faithful - Jason & Ashley	
				Transition: Welcome & Greet/Seat audience.	
4	10:17	11:47	1:17	**Video:** Roll-in (1)	6:47
5	10:18	11:48	1:18	**NS:** Message Part 1 (13)	6:48
6	10:31	12:01	1:31	**Video:** Amena Brown - In the Beginning (2)	7:01
7	10:33	12:03	1:33	**Worship Team (4)**	7:03
				Silent Night - Jason	
				Transition:	
8	10:37	12:07	1:37	**NS:** Message Part 2 (8)	7:07
9	10:45	12:15	1:45	**Drama:** Spoken Word (Scriptures) (2)	7:15
10	10:47	12:17	1:47	**Worship Team w/ Dance (4)**	7:17
				O Come O Come Emmanuel - Jason	
				Transition:	
11	10:51	12:21	1:51	**NS:** Message Con't./Prayer/Next Steps (11)	7:21
12	11:02	12:32	2:02	**NS:** Imp. Info/Offering (3)	7:32
				Service Ends	
13	11:05	12:35	2:05	**Music:** Let It Snow, Let It Snow, Let t Snow - Ella Fitzgerald	7:35

"vertical" message series

Notes from Pastor to Creative Team for Planning

Working definition: Prayer is personal communication with God.

March 19—Why Pray?

Followed by citywide prayer walk. Worship service held at Salvation Army. Simple introductory message on the power of prayer, why God wants us to pray, what happens when we pray, daily prayer and the Christian's life.

March 26—How to Pray for Myself

Praise and thanksgiving, praying God's will, understanding God's best (asking for what we want and trusting God to give us what's best), the Lord's Prayer (could use it as an element in the service), prayer of salvation/common grace (prayers God hears and answers before we are Christians), the posture of prayer.

April 2—How to Listen to God

Confession, God's Word speaks, fasting, when God is silent/ waiting on God, ask/seek/knock (push one-year Bible reading again).

April 9—How to Pray for Others (Palm Sunday/Communion)

Praying with others, the role of the Spirit in intercession, praying for salvation (talk about whom to invite to the Easter service).

(Growth Group testimony on how a group experienced an answered prayer, particularly a salvation request.)

General Thoughts

- Are we asking groups to do anything special leading up to Easter? Maybe add to their normal Holy Week gathering a special prayer time on whom to invite to Easter.
- Would we want to do a "Theology of Prayer in Three Hours or Less" seminar in early April?
- Twenty-four hours of prayer leading up to Easter. We could probably do 240 hours (ask everyone to sign up for one hour of prayer). We could even open the front room of the office during Holy Week (turn it into a prayer experience) and/or set aside a prayer room on Palm Sunday for people to use around the services.

Creative Planning Meeting Notes

March 19—Why Pray? (Nelson teaching)
- 11:00 a.m. pre-service concert
- Nine-minute "Hope Sunday" video
- Five-minute Mac Pier interview
- Citywide prayer walk after the service
- Adopt a child tables before and after (Elaina)
- 3:00 p.m. baptism
- Sermon: Acrostic of PRAY
  - Reminds me to pray
- Repackaged/edited prayer interviews
- Video clip: *Christmas Vacation*
- Song: "Higher" by Creed
- 90 percent of Americans believe in God (50 percent of them pray)

March 26—How to Pray for Myself (Kerrick teaching)
- Video clip: *Any Given Sunday*
- Walkout music: "Pray" by MC Hammer
- Q&A: The posture of prayer

- Prayer box: prayer stations with images of people praying. Attendees have the opportunity to write and post prayer requests at a station following the service.
- Video clip ideas
  - *Forrest Gump*
  - *Because of Winn Dixie*
- Moment in service to pray for self
- Previously at The Journey video before the message
- Thought: Boat and land . . . which come to which . . . man and God
- Song: "Hungry"

April 2—How to Listen to God (Nelson teaching)
- Video clip: *Bruce Almighty*
- Q&A: Does God speak audibly? (booming voice from offstage, comedy)
- Prayer box/photos around service
- Dance: open with the song "40" with dancers onstage
- Video clip ideas
  - *Forrest Gump*
  - *The Apostle*
  - *Bruce Almighty* car crash scene
  - *The Matrix*
- Moment in service to listen to God
- Possible drama

April 9—How to Pray for Others (Nelson teaching)
- 10:00 a.m. ordination ceremony for CB and JHK

- Possible Growth Group testimony on answered prayer
- Communion (Growth Group leaders to serve)
- Hand out Easter invitations to all in attendance
- Easter postcard in program: "Thank God It's Monday" series
- Moment in service to pray for others
- Video testimony: James
- Video clip ideas
  - *Bruce Almighty*
  - *We Were Soldiers*
- Q&A: Praise and thanksgiving (Whom do I pray to?)
  - John 17:1–26: Jesus prays for himself, for his disciples, for all believers
- Stats on people being prayed for (Chuck Colson)

April 16—Easter (Nelson teaching)
- Freebie resources on prayer DVD
- Simple service/quality service
- Clear focus on resurrection
- No choir

Miscellaneous Ideas
- Theological moment of reflection at each service
- Dancers during the worship set
- Painters spell out PRAY throughout the series
- Confession illustration of balloon and string
- Illustration: gossip and telephone game
- Bird in hands illustration

Message Research Schedule

Research Due the Monday Three Weeks before the Message

By Monday, February 27
March 19—Why Pray? (NS)

- Power of prayer
- Praying for my city
- Theology of prayer
- What happens in prayer?
- What happens to me in prayer?
- Lord's Prayer

By Monday, March 6
March 26—How to Pray for Myself (KT)

- Examples of praying for yourself in Scripture
- Prayer of salvation
- If God knows everything, why do I have to pray?
- Whom do I pray to and whose name do I pray in?
- Can I pray for trivial things? Does God care, hear?
- Is God going to answer my prayer, or is he going to do what's best for me?

By Monday, March 13
April 2—How to Listen to God (NS/CB)

- How do I hear God? What are the different ways?
- Biblical people who heard from God
- How can I know that it's God and not something I'm making up?
- Spending time with God daily
- Being thankful
- Getting away from others, being quiet
- Saying yes before we know what God wants us to do

By Monday, March 20
April 9—How to Pray for Others (NS)

- Praying for my friends and co-workers
- Inviting people to church
- How do I pray for others?
- Praying for another's salvation
- Praying specifically

Message Research Example

March 19—Why Pray?

Quotations

1. Real prayer is life creating and life changing. (Richard Foster)
2. Fear not because your prayer is stammering, your words feeble, and your language poor. Jesus can understand you. Just as a mother understands the first lisping of her infant, so does the blessed Savior understand sinners. He can read a sigh and see a meaning in a groan. (J. C. Ryle)
3. Prayer is self-surrender. (Gordon MacDonald)
4. We readily acknowledge that God alone is to be the rule and measure of our prayers. In our prayers we are to look totally unto Him and act totally for Him, and we must pray in this manner and for such ends as are suitable to His glory. (William Law)
5. Remember that God is our only sure trust. To Him, I commend you. . . . My son, neglect not the duty of secret prayer. (Mary Washington)
6. I've discovered it is not sufficient simply to try to take time for quietness but that I must, with all diligence, make time.

Whatever keeps me from prayer, solitude, and the Bible, however good it appears, is my enemy if I am to be God's devoted friend and follower. (Tommy Barnett)

7. Prayer is a strong wall and fortress of the church; it is a goodly Christian weapon. (Martin Luther)

8. God hears no more than the heart speaks; and if the heart be dumb, God will certainly be deaf. (Thomas Brooks)

9. Prayer as a relationship is probably your best indication about the health of your love relationship with God. If your prayer life has been slack, your love relationship has grown cold. (John Piper)

10. A sinning man will stop praying. A praying man will stop sinning. (Leonard Ravenhill)

11. God's answers are wiser than our prayers. (Unknown)

12. I was frustrated out of my mind, trying to figure out the will of God. I was doing everything but getting into the presence of God and asking Him to show me. (Paul Little)

13. Groanings that can't be uttered are often prayers that can't be refused. (Phillips Brooks)

14. Prayer is faith passing into action. (Richard Cecil)

15. Satan trembles when he sees the weakest saint upon his knees. (William Cowper)

Scripture

1 Timothy 2:2—[Pray this way] for kings and all others who are in authority, so that we can live in peace and quietness, in godliness and dignity.

2 Corinthians 1:11—He will rescue us because you are helping by praying for us. As a result, many will give thanks

to God because so many people's prayers for our safety have been answered.

Philippians 1:19—For I know that as you pray for me and as the Spirit of Jesus Christ helps me, this will all turn out for my deliverance.

Psalm 122:6—Pray for the peace of Jerusalem. May all who love this city prosper.

Isaiah 62:6—O Jerusalem, I have posted watchmen on your walls; they will pray to the LORD day and night for the fulfillment of his promises. Take no rest, all you who pray.

Ephesians 6:18—Pray at all times and on every occasion in the power of the Holy Spirit. Stay alert and be persistent in your prayers for all Christians everywhere.

1 Timothy 2:1—I urge you, first of all, to pray for all people. As you make your requests, plead for God's mercy upon them, and give thanks.

Luke 7:2–3—Now the highly valued slave of a Roman officer was sick and near death. When the officer heard about Jesus, he sent some respected Jewish leaders to ask him to come and heal his slave.

Romans 10:1—Dear brothers and sisters, the longing of my heart and my prayer to God is that the Jewish people might be saved.

James 5:14—Are any among you sick? They should call for the elders of the church and have them pray over them, anointing them with oil in the name of the Lord.

Matthew 5:44—But I say, love your enemies! Pray for those who persecute you!

Numbers 12:13—So Moses cried out to the Lord, "Heal her, O God, I beg you!"

James 5:16—Confess your sins to each other and pray for each other so that you may be healed. The earnest prayer of a righteous person has great power and produces wonderful results.

1 John 5:16—If you see a Christian brother or sister sinning in a way that does not lead to death, you should pray, and God will give that person life. But there is a sin that leads to death, and I am not saying you should pray for those who commit it.

Ephesians 3:14–17—When I think of the wisdom and scope of God's plan, I fall to my knees and pray to the Father, the Creator of everything in heaven and on earth. I pray that from his glorious, unlimited resources he will give you mighty inner strength through his Holy Spirit. And I pray that Christ will be more and more at home in your hearts as you trust in him. May your roots go down deep into the soil of God's marvelous love.

Psalm 5:3—Listen to my voice in the morning, Lord. Each morning I bring my requests to you and wait expectantly.

notes

1. Pat MacMillan, *The Performance Factor: Unlocking the Secrets of Teamwork* (Nashville: Broadman & Holman, 2001), xiii.

2. Stephen R. Covey, *The Seven Habits of Highly Effective People* (New York: Free Press, 2004), 98.

3. Andy Stanley and Ronald Lane Jones, *Communicating for a Change* (Sisters, OR: Multnomah, 2006).

4. Michael Green, *Evangelism in the Early Church* (Grand Rapids: Eerdmans, 1970), 276.

5. MacMillan, *Performance Factor*, 72.

6. Ken Blanchard, *Leading at a Higher Level* (Upper Saddle River, NJ: Prentice Hall, 2007), 149.

7. Ibid., 260.

We hope this book will become a conversation starter between us. We are constantly developing resources and gathering ideas from others to help you lead your church in worship. In fact, we recently held a private event for our coaching alumni where we taught everything we know about worship planning (it would fill at least three books like this one) called "The Planning Worship Services for Life Transformation Workshop." You can find information about securing the recording of this workshop at this book's website:

www.ChurchLeaderInsights.com/Engage

You can also use the website to connect with us. We would love to hear your story and to continue discussing the ways we can grow together for God's glory.

Your partners in ministry,

Nelson Searcy
Lead Pastor, The Journey Church
www.JourneyMetro.com
Founder, www.ChurchLeader
Insights.com

Jason Hatley
Pastor of Worship Arts, The Journey Church
www.JourneyMetro.com
www.WorshipLeaderInsights.com

Nelson Searcy is the founding lead pastor of The Journey Church of the City with locations in New York City, Queens, Brooklyn, and Boca Raton, FL. He is also the founder of www.ChurchLeaderInsights.com. He and his church appear routinely on lists such as the 50 Most Influential Churches and the 25 Most Innovative Leaders. Searcy lives in New York City.

Jennifer Dykes Henson is a freelance writer based in New York City. She has served as a writer/producer and ministry consultant to organizations across the East Coast. Prior to moving to New York, Jennifer worked with Dr. Charles Stanley as the manager of marketing communications for In Touch Ministries in Atlanta, Georgia.

Jason Hatley is the Pastor of Worship Arts at The Journey Church and has been a worship leader since 1996. Jason was a part of The Journey's original launch team. He built from scratch The Journey's Worship Arts Team, a group of over 200 artists and technicians who develop and implement The Journey's creative and technical elements at the weekly Sunday service. Currently, Jason serves as the Pastor of Worship Arts at The Journey's newest location in Boca Raton, FL. Jason is the Founder of www.WorshipLeaderInsights.com. He has spoken at the Willow Creek Arts Conference, The Purpose Driven Worship Conference, as well as seminars around the country. He has a B.M. in Sacred Music Performance from Appalachian State University.

NEW FROM NELSON SEARCY

FOR YOU AND YOUR CHURCH

Maximize is the ultimate how-to book for pastors and church leaders who long for their churches to be fully resourced and able to carry out ministry initiatives without financial strain. Shining a light on the often taboo subject of money, *Maximize* offers an innovative, step-by-step plan for systemizing and maximizing financial gifts while growing strong disciples.

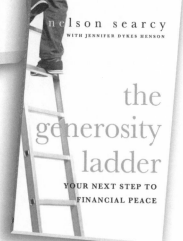

Published alongside *Maximize* is Searcy's book *The Generosity Ladder*, for anyone who desires to handle money with excellence. Written to answer all of the questions and misunderstandings that surround the intersection of God and money, *The Generosity Ladder* will allow laypeople to fully grasp God's plan for their finances.

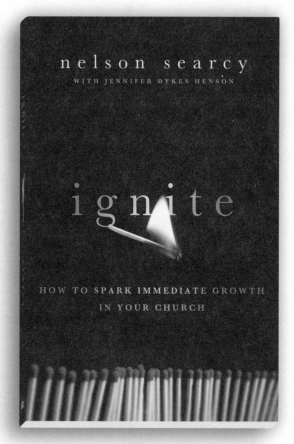

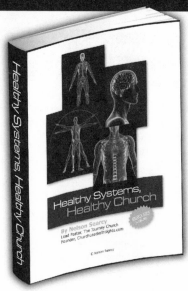